YOUR LEGAL RIGHTS AS A minor

LINCOLN
Revised Edition

YOUR LEGAL RIGHTS AS A minor

BY ROBERT H. LOEB, JR.

in consultation with
John P. Maloney

JAN '80 7.90

Franklin Watts
New York | London | 1978

I wish to express my thanks and appreciation to
Howard T. Walker, law librarian at the Connecticut
State Library, for his patient assistance in
uncovering the mysteries of legal source material.
Robert H. Loeb, Jr.

The material contained in this book is
offered only as information for the general
public and should not be regarded as legal
advice or opinion. The reader should consult
his lawyer in every case where he has a
specific problem or question requiring legal
assistance.

The authors wish to thank the following for permission to quote:
The Lawyers Co-operative Publishing Co.
for material from *American Jurisprudence Second*
and West Publishing Company
for material from *Corpus Juris Secundum*.

Library of Congress Cataloging in Publication Data

Loeb, Robert H.
    Your legal rights as a minor.

    Bibliography: p.
    Includes index.
    SUMMARY: Discusses the origin, purpose, and
application of the most relevant legal rights of
minors in the United States.
    1. Children—Law—United States—Juvenile litera-
ture. [1. Law. 2. Children's rights] I. Maloney, John
P., joint author. II. Title.
KF479.Z9L6   1978   346'.73'013   78-7856
ISBN 0-531-02231-5

CONTENTS

YOUR LEGAL RIGHTS AS A minor

INTRODUCTION

A Minor's Guide to Legal Rights

Before writing this book I talked to a number of junior and senior high school students to find out what they would like to know about their legal rights. At first, many of these young people were suspicious and asked me, "Is this going to be another one of those books telling us how to behave properly?"

In case you have similar doubts, the answer is "No." The way things are legally has little to do with personal opinion or morality.

The way things are legally may not be the way you think things ought to be. But the difference between *knowing* your legal rights and *not knowing* them will, I hope, make a difference. It should help you to handle many problems, frustrations, and troubles which confront young Americans today. Wishful thinking, or guessing about your legal rights is as futile as trying to play a complicated game without knowing the rules. You're almost certain to lose.

The laws about minors are rules which society has established, in a hit-or-miss fashion, over hundreds of years. Many of these laws will seem old-fashioned and out-of-date. That's because many of them are. Others may seem unjust, discriminatory, and restrictive. In some cases they are just as bad as they seem. However, underlying many of the laws about minors is this basic motivation: to protect you. You will understand this more clearly as you read about the origins of some of these laws.

I believe you will find that some of them are not as restrictive as they may seem—or as some of your elders might like you to believe they are. The purpose of this book is to present you with the legal facts of life so that you can function constructively and effectively, rather than desperately or despairingly, during the years of your minority.

Our reason for interviewing young people first was to avoid writing about what *we* thought minors wanted to know. Instead, we wished to learn first-hand what is really of interest to you about your legal rights. The students we interviewed came from varying economic and ethnic backgrounds: ghetto areas in large cities; upper-income suburbia; and rural areas where farming is still a dominant way of life.

Interests varied accordingly. For example, students from urban poverty areas were not exactly crying out for information about their rights to buy and sell stocks and bonds. Those from the rural areas were not as interested in knowing what their rights would be if they were arrested. However, all shared certain basic interests: parents' rights, school rights, marriage laws, driving regulations, drug laws, and commercial restrictions, among others.

This book does not claim to cover all the legal angles; rather we focus on those which seem to be most relevant. Moreover, even as this book was written, laws were changing—as they always will. For example, some states are modifying their drug laws. Abortion laws continue to be altered by courts and legislation. Criminal laws pertaining to minors are frequently revised.

The majority of laws pertaining both to minors and adults are local, state or federal laws called statutes. (See page 22 for definition of "statute.") Where it seems essential, we have listed particular statutes state by state. However, in most cases, we depend upon the fact that the laws affecting minors are very much the same throughout the land.

What is the origin of the legal concept *minor*? Who is a minor and why is there such a category under the law? The concept originates with British common law as it was written 150 years ago, and this thinking still applies today:

> In order to prevent, as far as possible, the evils which would arise from the imbecility and inexperience to which every man is subject on his entrance into the world, the legislature has imposed on him, for a given period, those disabilities, and embued him with those privileges, which, with their modification, are implied in the legal acceptation of the term *infant;* and every person is, in our law, considered as an infant, until he has completed the age of twenty-one years . . .[1]

The carryover of the term "infant" from nineteenth-century England to twentieth-century United

[1] Peregrine Bingham, *The Law of Infancy and Coverture* (London: J. Butterworth, 1816).

States holds both in definition and in purpose. You, a minor, are still referred to as an infant in many legal documents and statutes. In general, the same restrictions are imposed upon you today because of your alleged disabilities: namely, inexperience and consequent vulnerability—called "imbecility" in those days.

It may strike you as "imbecilic" that, even though all "infants" of eighteen can vote in federal elections, they are not always legally considered adults in other areas. For example: all states have lowered the age of majority from twenty-one, but not all have lowered it to eighteen. Furthermore, even though the age of majority in a state may be eighteen for one purpose, such as the purchase of liquor, the age of majority may remain higher for other purposes. And there are other areas of confusion well exemplified by the following passage:

> In our federal system, age of majority laws are within the province of the States. Therefore, such laws vary from one State to another. Majority laws are scattered throughout the statutes. Oftentimes, new laws have been adopted without giving sufficient consideration to reconciling them with existing ones. For example, a report of the Alaska Legislative Council in 1966 states: "In Alaska, a twenty-one-year-old borough assemblyman or city councilman who may incorporate a cooperative, devise a will, convey land and donate his eyes to a hospital, must have the written consent of his parents to get married." [2]

[2] Council of State Governments, *The Age of Majority*, 1972, p. 5.

Alaska has since rectified this oddity, but many people feel that such changes in the law take place far too slowly. There is a strong possibility that those with the power to make and interpret the laws want to preserve the old ways whether they are justified or not. However, there is another reason: laws simply cannot be in a constant state of change, for then no one would know where he or she stood. This does not excuse what is out-of-date, absurd, or inconsistent in many of our state laws, but time and thought are also needed in order to avoid chaos.

You may suspect, perhaps correctly, that your rights are also limited because the older generation wants to keep you under control. However, it is obvious that restrictions placed upon your commercial rights, for example, are essentially for your own protection and not for policing you. A minor is usually inexperienced in business. He would be easy prey for unscrupulous persons in the commercial world. Even adults are vulnerable, in this respect, because laws regulating business procedure are lax.

A more serious factor is that our laws are, in general, far more concerned with property rights than with human rights, and that rich people enjoy more immunity under the law than poor people. However, to offer a ray of hope, things have improved somewhat in this respect. Some quotations from a book written in 1909 give a grim picture of the laws then pertaining to child labor and employer liability. Although it was written by an English jurist and is chiefly concerned with British common law, it also shows the legal and social attitudes of the time, both in England and in the United States.

> An infant servant is within the common law rule that the master is not liable for injuries occurring in the ordinary course of his employment.
>
> Whereas a master employs an inexperienced workman upon dangerous work, it is his duty to instruct and caution him; but the master may delegate that duty to a competent person, and if he does so, he will not be liable for an injury to the workman resulting from the negligence of the delegate in not properly instructing or cautioning him . . .[3]

What does this reveal? Workers, regardless of age, were given scant protection. The "master's" only responsibility was to see to it that every worker was "instructed" and "cautioned." A child of ten or eleven who lost an arm or leg at work had no more legal recourse than an adult with much greater experience. This is a chilling example of property rights coming before human rights. Here is another example from the same book:

> An infant cannot, any more than an adult, recover damages if the injury has been caused by his negligence. . . . So where a child of three and one half years old got on a railway and was injured, no negligence being shown against the company, they were not liable.[4]

---

[3] A. H. Simpson, *Infant and Servant* (London, 1909).
[4] *Ibid.*

At common law, "infants" were offered certain protections because of their lack of mature judgment, but not when it came to protecting the property rights of the railway.

Today there are a number of laws and regulations that are supposed to protect minors by barring them from certain activities permitted to adults. For example, they are not allowed to attend X-rated movies or purchase pornographic books and magazines. For adults, these prohibitions would be considered a violation of constitutional rights under the Bill of Rights. Someday, perhaps, minors may challenge such restrictions for identical reasons.

One common complaint of many of the students we interviewed was that they were barred from certain types of jobs solely because of their age. This applied especially to students who attended technical schools. They felt that they were sufficiently experienced in operating certain types of machinery, yet were not allowed to put their knowledge and skills to profitable use because they were minors. As some of them said, "Under the law, we can't even operate an elevator!"

A more realistic complaint, however, might be that it has taken so long to give minors needed protection against labor exploitation and from being exposed to dangerous work. Prior to 1850, U.S. laws prohibiting children under ten from working up to twelve hours a day in factories under hazardous conditions were just about nonexistent. If that seems too long ago to be relevant, consider that it wasn't until

1950 that federal regulations specified a minimum age of sixteen for certain types of work. During World War II, in America, three and a half million children between the ages of fourteen and seventeen were working in factories under conditions that were less than good. However, corporate profits from this "war effort" were very good indeed.

In the past, millions of children nine years old and under were put to work in the fields instead of going to school. They weren't working because they were bored with school and preferred being in the great outdoors from dawn to dusk; they did it because they were compelled to. In most cases, this was rank exploitation. Only after 1950 did federal regulations prohibit hiring children under sixteen to work on farms. Even today, in some states this protection does not apply to children working for their parents or farming within the state. But in general, employment laws governing minors are at least a step closer to placing human rights ahead of profit and property rights.

For you to understand why certain laws pertaining to your rights exist, we shall occasionally cite from specific case histories. Often we shall quote directly from the statutes. In this way you will have a better understanding of why certain laws exist and you will learn some legal vocabulary. This should help you to understand such things as contracts and sales agreements on your own. In short, you will have a better picture of what the score really is.

Once again, the purpose of this book is not to

tell you how to behave, but rather to give you the facts about your legal rights and limitations as minors. This should enable you to make sounder decisions and to take more constructive action.

CHAPTER ONE

Wheeling— Driving Rights and Restrictions

If a constitutional amendment were suddenly passed barring anyone under twenty-one years of age from operating a motor vehicle, there would probably be a violent revolution within a few days' time. More than fifteen million furious young Americans would rise up and rebel with the burning conviction that one of their most important rights had been taken away from them.

So great is the lure of wheels in America that in 1970 there were 11.3 million licensed drivers aged twenty or under, and undoubtedly there are several million more as of this writing. Such is the fascination with automobiles in the United States that many students in their teens would probably prefer to flunk a final exam than to fail their driver's test. Every group of students we interviewed was extremely interested in knowing rights and restrictions concerning driving. The following information is offered as a result of the most frequently asked questions.

What are the age requirements for obtaining a driver's license in each state?

In case you are going to do interstate driving, it is important to know this: a licensed sixteen-year-old Connecticut driver, if driving in New York City, would be driving without a valid license because there the

age minimum is seventeen. This technicality might become a very unpleasant reality for a sixteen-year-old
driver involved in an accident. Here, then, is a listing
of the age limits by state:

Motor Vehicle Drivers' Ages

Source: Federal Highway Adm.

State, 1976	Driver's Age Jan 1, 1976 (1) Regular	(2) Juvenile	State, 1976	Driver's Age Jan 1, 1976 (1) Regular	(2) Juvenile
Alabama	16		Nebraska	16	14
Alaska	16		Nevada	16	14
Arizona	16		New Hampshire	16/18	16
Arkansas	16		New Jersey	17	16
California	16/18	14	New Mexico	15/16	
Colorado	21	16	New York	17/18	16
Connecticut	16/18		North Carolina	16/18	
Delaware	16/18		North Dakota	16	14
Florida	16/18		Ohio	16/18	14
Georgia	16		Oklahoma	16	
Hawaii	15		Oregon	16	14
Idaho	16	14	Pennsylvania	17/18	16
Illinois	16/18		Rhode Island	16/18	
Indiana	16/18		South Carolina	16	15
Iowa	16/18	14	South Dakota	16	14
Kansas	16	14	Tennessee	16	14
Kentucky	16		Texas	16/18	15
Louisiana	17	15	Utah	16	
Maine	15/17	15	Vermont	18	16
Maryland	16/18		Virginia	16/18	
Massachusetts	18	16½	Washington	16/18	
Michigan	16/18	14	West Virginia	16/18	
Minnesota	16/18	15	Wisconsin	16/18	14
Mississippi	15		Wyoming	16	14
Missouri	16		District of Columbia	18	16
Montana	15/16				

(1) Unrestricted operation of private passenger car. When 2 ages are shown,
license is issued at lower age upon completion of approved driver education course.
(2) Juvenile license issued for use between home and school in Cal., Iowa, Kan.,
Me., Mich., Neb., Nev., N.H., N.D., Oreg.; restricted to daylight or curfew hours in
Idaho, Ill., La., Mass., Minn., N.Y., Pa., S.C., S.D., Tenn., Wis.; hardship cases in
Ohio and Texas; for agricultural pursuits in N.J.

Is there compulsory auto insurance liability coverage for minors?

Those states listed below require liability insurance for everyone; other states did not require this coverage as of 1977: *

California	Minnesota
Colorado	Nevada
Connecticut	New Jersey
Delaware	New York
Florida	North Carolina
Georgia	North Dakota
Hawaii	Pennsylvania
Idaho	Puerto Rico
Kansas	Rhode Island—
Kentucky	for minors only
Maryland	South Carolina
Massachusetts	Utah
Michigan	Virgin Islands

* Source—Nov. 1973, American Insurance Association. As of June 1977, no change.

Regardless of state law, what risks do minors subject themselves to if they drive an uninsured car— whether their own or someone else's?

In case of accident, where you are at fault and where property damage and/or personal injury is involved, you will be personally liable. This means that whatever property you may own—money in a savings account, money in a checking account, the car itself if you own it—can be taken from you to satisfy your liability. But far more serious is that your wages can be "attached" (a portion of them can be taken from you) if and when you get a job, and this attachment will remain in effect until the judgment is paid in full. You might, in other words, be paying off this debt for many years or even for the rest of your life.

Why are insurance rates for minors so much higher than for adults?

Insurance companies base car insurance rates on accident statistics. Although the rates vary with individual insurance companies, in general people up to twenty-five years of age (sometimes even thirty) pay more—far more—than their elders, because of these accident statistics. In 1971 drivers under twenty (10.2 percent of all drivers) were involved in 14.9 percent of all fatal accidents, and in 16.6 percent of all accidents. Drivers twenty to twenty-four (11.1 percent of all drivers) were involved in 19 percent of all fatal accidents, and in 18.1 percent of all accidents.

As a rule, why do male minors have to pay higher insurance premiums than female minors?

No, it's not because of women's liberation; again it's based upon accident statistics. The average rate of accident involvement was higher for young men than for young women from 1958 through 1970.

When can minors qualify for lower insurance premiums?

1. When a minor marries, the rate decreases. This is not because insurance companies are trying to promote marriage; the lower rate is based on accident statistics. Married people are involved in fewer accidents than are singles.

2. When a minor passes an approved driver's education course (through his local school system), the rate can decrease as much as 25 percent, depending on the individual insurance company.

3. There is a "good student" discount recog-

nized by some insurance companies. This usually means being in the upper 20 percent of your class. Obviously, you must furnish proof of this in writing.

What are your liabilities, in case of accident, while taking a driver's education lesson?

In general, all driver's education vehicles are covered for accidents; this insurance also covers the student driver.

What can happen to you if you are arrested for a driving violation out of state?

The arresting officer can take you to the police station where you will be required to put up a sum of money as bond to ensure your appearance at trial. The payment is always required in cash, and the amount is usually the amount of the fine that you would pay if you were to plead guilty to the offense in court. Then, if you don't show up, the money is retained as the fine. If you cannot meet the cash requirement, there is this alternative: you can ask to "post a bond." This means getting in touch with a bondsman who, for a fee, will furnish a legal certificate (bond) which guarantees that if you fail to appear, the court can cash in the bond. A parent or other reliable adult must sign the bond; as a minor you are not permitted to sign it yourself. If you or the car are covered by insurance, the insurance company pays for the premium on the bond (within limits), but not for the bond itself. It is important to have your insurance policy number or that of the owner of the car at hand for immediate verification. Just giving the name of the insured person will not help much since it takes many days to trace a policy without having its number. Again, remember that no bondsman will post bond directly for you.

If you borrow a car (either with tacit or explicit permission) and are involved in an accident that is your fault, what liabilities are involved?

1. Basically, the owner of the car is liable along with the driver for accidents caused by the driver's negligence.

2. If the owner does not have insurance, but your own parents carry car insurance, their policy may cover your liability.

3. In case of no insurance, the courts usually hold the driver and the owner equally liable. This means that you could be held responsible for paying the entire amount due.

4. Insurance does not protect you against criminal suit. If the accident took place because of reckless driving on your part, or while you were driving under the influence of alcohol or drugs, you are liable to criminal prosecution.

5. If you wreck the borrowed car and the owner does not carry collision insurance, it is up to you to pay for the damage. If he carries $100 or $250 deductible collision insurance, you are responsible for making up this out-of-pocket cost. Insurance companies have the right to seek repayment of the entire sum by the driver even if the owner carries insurance.

What steps should you take in case of an accident?

Here is what insurance companies advise:

1. If there are witnesses, try to get their names and addresses.

2. Don't admit responsibility for the accident to anyone and make no other statement regarding it to anyone except the police.

3. Contact your insurance agent or the owner's insurance agent as soon as possible.

4. When someone has been injured, every state requires that you fill out a form to that effect within a specified length of time and that you file it with the state's bureau of motor vehicles.

5. When there is no bodily injury but there is damage to property of over $100 to $300 (depending on the state), a form describing the damage must be filled in and sent to the bureau of motor vehicles. The police will usually remind you of this (but don't depend on it). Your insurance adjuster will always remind you.

Can minors rent a car if they are licensed to drive?

The answer to this is "No." No national car rental agency will rent a car to anyone under eighteen. If a parent or other obliging adult rents a car in his name and allows you to drive it, he or she is not covered by the car rental company's insurance in case of accident. Thus the person who rented the car becomes personally and totally liable if you have an accident.

CHAPTER TWO

Dealing— Commercial Rights and Restrictions

**Real Estate, Buying and Selling Goods,
Banking, Stocks and Bonds,
Wills, Business Ventures, Credit Cards**

Before answering specific questions about minors' commercial rights, it is important to explain the legal reasoning underlying such rights and limitations. Why is it that minors (often referred to as "infants" in the various statutes governing them) find it difficult, if not impossible, to enter into many kinds of business transactions? It comes to this: in general minors cannot legally be held to a contract—so no one wants to deal with them.

The fact that you may legally be termed an "infant" should provide you with a clue. Both *common law* and *statutes* attempt to protect "infants" from exploitation by adults. The law assumes that youthful impetuousness and lack of experience in dealing in the marketplace could make you easy prey for profit-hungry business people.

Common law is not law specifically passed by legislatures. Rather, it is law based upon judges' decisions that have set a precedent for future legal decisions.

A statute is a law passed by a legislative body, whether local, state, or federal. Most of your commercial rights and restrictions are regulated by your state legislature. The aim of these statutes is to protect you rather than to restrict you without reason. They are designed to discourage adults from engaging in certain kinds of business transactions with you, a minor. And this is accomplished very simply: as a general rule, you as a minor cannot bind yourself by a contract. In other words, your signature on such documents as a bill of sale, a lease, or a loan agreement is not binding.

Stated in another way, this is your privilege as a minor: by law you can duck out of, or disavow, a business deal. Consequently, business firms and individuals frequently will not do business with you because they realize they cannot recover anything under the law if you change your mind on a deal or find it impossible to make payment.

As the law has developed in the different states, it has refined this general rule that minors cannot be held responsible for contracts. A number of important exceptions have emerged. One limits the means by which a minor can get out of a contract. In some states, the minor must wait until he or she has reached the age of majority and then must act quickly to escape from the contract. (In other states, the minor can act immediately, without waiting for age of majority, to void a contract.) A more important variation has been enacted in some states, whereby the minor is required to return any goods received, before getting a refund.

Still another important exception concerns contracts a minor makes involving what the law calls "necessaries." These contracts are considered valid and cannot be voided. In the area of "necessaries" a minor is personally liable and cannot go back on a contract. The result is that individuals or business firms may be willing to enter into direct sales negotiations with minors, knowing that they are protected by law.

But what is a "necessary" and why has this exception been made? If we trace this idea back to its source, we understand it better. Here, we shall quote directly from *American Jurisprudence Second,* which is what one might call an encyclopedia of law in the United States. Throughout the book we shall also quote from another reference work, *Corpus Juris Secundum,* a similar work. Each of these legal "encyclopedias" consists of approximately forty volumes, and each volume is over 1,000 pages long. They are used by lawyers, judges, and legislators to check on any aspect of law from its origin to the present.

American Jurisprudence Second has this to say about "necessaries."

> According to the rule laid down by Lord Coke [an eminent British barrister of the early seventeenth century] an infant may bind himself to pay for his meat, drink, apparel, necessary physic, and other such necessaries, and likewise for his good teaching or instruction whereby he may profit himself afterward. This, generally speaking, has been accepted as the true doctrine. About such elementary necessities of life as food, raiment, and lodging, if the infant lacks

them and the amount and quality are reasonable, there can be no question.

. . . An agreement to purchase a number of items of household goods and furnishings, including a stove and a bedroom set, has been held a contract for necessaries where a minor was married and living with his wife and child at the time of the delivery of the articles.

. . . In several cases a horse has been held not to be a necessary. As to whether an infant's contract for employment may be deemed a contract for necessaries where the employer agrees to furnish board and lodging as part payment for the services rendered, the decisions are not in agreement.[1]

There it is, the underlying philosophy of the law pertaining to your commercial rights. It stems from the seventeenth century. Even the reference to whether a horse can be considered a "necessary" has a direct bearing on your ability to buy a car today, as you will see.

With this as background let us take up the questions that apply directly to you. In reading the answers to the following questions, however, it is important to be aware of two things. First, what is considered a "necessary" for Tom or Dick may not be considered a "necessary" for Harry or Jane. It depends on the individual circumstances. Second, in the commercial area the question is not so much one of your legal rights; the question is whether others are willing to do business with you in light of your

[1] *American Jurisprudence Second*, Vol. 42, Paragraph 69, p. 71.

special privileges as a minor. The fact that you are not bound by contract can make people unwilling to buy from you, sell or lease to you, or make you a bank loan.

How easy is it for minors to lease a room, apartment, or house?

It is not easy. Minors cannot realistically count on being able to enter into a rental contract on their own. Usually they will have to have a parent, guardian, or some other adult sign the lease.

Under ordinary circumstances in order to rent, one signs a lease agreement. This is a contract. And a minor can void it or back out of it. If you do void the lease agreement and can show proof that you did not use the premises as a "necessary," or did not use them at all, you can get back whatever rent you paid.

On the other hand, where your rental *was* a "necessary," you might be held liable for a reasonable rent—so a landlord might be more willing to rent to you. For example, if you rented a room in a college town in order to attend the college, this would come under the category of a "necessary" because it was for the purpose of enabling you to further your education. However, the landlord is still taking a risk— for, unlike an adult, you would not be liable for the balance of the lease if you moved out before its termination.

To make it even more risky for the landlord, the

law in some localities states that minors under the age of eighteen *cannot* make a contract relating to real property (such as housing or real estate). According to these laws, any such contract entered into by minors under eighteen is automatically void and does not require any action by you to make it void. Obviously, if this is the law of the locality where you wish to sign a lease, the landlord will not go through the useless act of having you sign a contract which he knows is invalid.

How easy is it for minors to buy or sell real estate?

As a minor, you should assume that you cannot buy or sell real estate in your own right. It is just as difficult as renting property, and for the same reasons. Let us assume that you have the funds and want to buy an A-frame lodge in a skiing area. The owner, or his lawyer, knows that your signature to the sales agreement has no legal standing and, as a minor, you can void your contract at any time. Moreover, buying a house in a ski area cannot ordinarily be considered a "necessary." If the owner sold you his house, you could occupy it, and even damage it, and then void the contract and demand the return of the money. And you would be entitled to it by law. (On the other hand, if you were earning your living as a ski instructor, the purchase of the lodge to live in might be classified as a "necessary" and you could therefore be held to the contract. Then the owner might be willing to sell to you.) Normally and understandably, however, most property owners do not wish to take the risks of selling to a minor.

How easy is it for minors to buy things (other than motor vehicles)?

The answer to this depends on two variables. First, are you paying cash or buying on credit? Second, what are you buying?

Let us say you buy a pair of skis from a sporting goods store for $100 cash. After trying out the skis for several days, you find them "unsatisfactory" mainly because you damaged one against a tree. You return them to the store and ask for your money back. The store is legally bound to refund your money in full despite the damage. Why? Because any sale is a contractual arrangement and you, being a minor, have the right to void it. (Even so, minors usually have little difficulty in buying things for cash—partly because such purchases usually do not involve as much money as purchases of real estate or motor vehicles, partly because people, minors included, usually make such purchases in good faith.)

Now, let us assume that you have only half the cash necessary to buy the skis and ask to pay the balance in weekly installments. Let's say you have a job, and offer that as proof of your ability to pay. If the store owner agrees to the sale under these conditions and you don't meet the payments, he will have no legal way to collect the balance you owe. Why? Because, as a minor, you can void your contract.

This is why it is difficult for minors to purchase things on credit. In fact, even if you falsified your age to buy the skis on credit, you might still be able to void the deal unless it could be proven that you meant to cheat. (Some states do have laws which automatically consider such actions fraudulent, thus making a minor liable.)

Now let us examine the second variable: the nature of the thing you are buying. You will recall that if something is deemed a "necessary," you have the same legal obligations as an adult. This means that if you buy clothing, medicine, food, educational supplies, or medical care, and it can be proven that you need it, you are responsible for payment. Thus, when the sale involves "necessaries," the seller is protected. This makes it somewhat easier to obtain credit to buy certain items.

In conclusion, buying things for cash is not difficult for a minor, despite the fact that he or she can't be held to a contract. However, credit is difficult for a minor to obtain. This applies even to "necessaries" because they are subject to so many varying definitions.

How about selling things (other than motor vehicles)?

Sellings things usually presents no problem despite the fact that sales by a minor are subject to the same rules and consequent uncertainties—this time for the buyer. For example, suppose you sell a pair of skis to an adult for cash. Several days later, for some reason, you change your mind and repossess the skis in the absence of their new owner. He then comes and demands that you return the cash he paid you. But you have already spent half the money. The remainder is all he can recover.

However, in practice, few adults are apt to worry about a minor's rights to reclaim an article. This is perhaps because few adults are aware of your technical right to go back on the sale; and perhaps because most adults assume you are making the sale in good faith.

How easy is it for minors to buy a car, truck, or motorcycle?

Even for cash, minors usually cannot get a dealer to sell them a car; most automobile dealers are unwilling to take the risks involved. They will insist that the car be purchased in the name of your parent or guardian or some other adult.

As a general rule, a motor vehicle is not regarded as a "necessary," and therefore a minor may disaffirm (or go back on) the purchase and get a refund of the full price. However, a trend is developing in the law: when a motor vehicle is used for something more than simply pleasure-driving, it may be considered a "necessary." In a 1971 case, for example, the Supreme Court of Oklahoma stated: "In our opinion, private transportation secured by a minor in aid of his quest for a livelihood should be considered a necessity." In that particular case the minor used his car to drive to and from his job, and that was sufficient in the court's opinion to consider it a necessity for which he could be bound to his contract.

In fact, however, minors can almost always void car purchase contracts—even when the car was used for work. This means that theoretically you could purchase a car for cash, wreck it the following day, return it to the dealer, and demand the return of your money even though the car was damaged.

Nevertheless, there are a few car dealers who will take the risk. Neither of you is breaking the law; the dealer is merely taking a huge chance.

How easy is it for minors to open a checking or savings account and deposit or withdraw funds without parental consent?

It should be just as easy for you to open a checking or savings account, in your own name, as it is for an adult.

Minors may deposit money in a bank (in either a checking or savings account) and reclaim it at any time, even during their minority. The bank cannot be sued by a parent or guardian for returning a minor's money to him or her. However, if you are in your early teens, a bank would probably investigate to make certain that the funds are yours and it would probably check up on your family's economic status.

How easy is it for minors to get a bank loan?

Once again, because they have "contractual immunity," minors can void their contracts to repay borrowed money. This effectively discourages banks from lending them money. Technically a minor could not get out of paying back a loan for "necessaries," or to pay off debts for "necessaries," but banks still shy away from making loans to minors even for such purposes.

One important exception concerns loans made for educational purposes. Many states have special laws which allow minors to be bound by loans made to pay for tuition, board, room, books, etc., at school or college. This means you are legally bound to pay back the loan. This is actually to your advantage because banks in those states are willing to lend money to minors for such purposes.

With the exception of educational loans, most banks will not make loans to minors whether or not the money is required for "necessaries." However, a few banks will take the calculated risks involved. For example, a chain of thirty-one banks in Massachusetts will loan up to $200 to minors—provided, of course, that the minor has a satisfactory financial record. They issue what might be termed "Junior Credit Cards." Therefore, if you are refused loan credit by one bank solely because you are a minor, it may be worth shopping around for a bank that will make an exception.

How easy is it for minors to obtain gas credit cards or other credit cards?

Here again, minors are handicapped by their contractual immunity: since they can't be held to a contract, no one wants to deal with them.

At the present time, no gasoline company will

make any exceptions. This means it is impossible for you to obtain such a credit card. The same applies to other types of credit cards.

How easy is it for minors to buy stocks and bonds?

Again, because of a minor's ability, or "privilege," to disavow a contract, no brokerage firm will accept an order to buy or sell securities from a minor. You will find it almost impossible to deal in securities. The only exceptions which have been made were made in error. It's "No" when it comes to buying and selling stocks and bonds.

How easy is it for minors to engage in a business venture?

According to common law, and where there is no specific statute modifying it, minors engaging in business are not contractually responsible. If a statute does exist that permits you to engage in a business or profession, then you are contractually liable if the business is your livelihood and not just a means of earning extra spending money. In addition, the business must be your own, and under some statutes you must obtain a license to engage in it.

This implies that, depending upon the existing statutes in the area where you live, it may be possible for you to set up a business or to engage in a profession if you earn your living by it. However, since starting and operating a business usually requires credit, minors are severely handicapped. It will be hard for a minor to get the necessary credit.

How easy is it for minors to obtain bail on their own?

Minors cannot be held liable for breach of contract for bail. For this reason minors will find it impossible to obtain bail on their own. Consequently, an adult must sign the bail bond and make himself responsible for you.

How easy is it for minors to make a valid will?

This may seem an unlikely concern for most minors; but it is possible for a minor to possess funds or property acquired through inheritance, or from winning a state lottery, or by saving money earned through employment. It is also possible that under certain circumstances such minors might not want their wealth to go to their parents or brothers and sisters if they should die, but rather to someone else or to some cause. What can a minor do about this? The early common law allowed a boy of fourteen and a girl of twelve to execute a valid will (write a will that would hold up legally). Today however, statutes in most localities give the right to execute a valid will only to those who have reached at least the age of eighteen.

In general, then, minors cannot make valid wills. However, if you have money or property, check with a lawyer to learn what the specific statute is where you live. If it is impossible for you to make a valid will, your property would automatically go to your next of kin upon your death.

CHAPTER THREE

Sex and Society— Sexual Rights and Restrictions

It is easy to understand why the law—both common and statutory—regulates commercial dealings, employment, the operation of motor vehicles, and so forth. But the law for many centuries has also concerned itself very much with the most personal and private relationship between people: sexual conduct. This includes sexual conduct between men and women and sexual conduct between people of the same sex.

The many and various laws covering sex, as with most of our other laws, have roots embedded in the past, mainly in the Christian ethics of the Middle Ages. At that time, the Church was the supreme arbiter of human conduct—especially regarding sexual relationships. Consequently, much of the common law and many of the statutes on our books today stem from ancient beliefs that are still reverently preserved. Trying to change them often seems as difficult as changing the Bible. Tampering with such laws in order to make them more relevant to our current lives always arouses powerful emotions.

For example, it was not until January 2, 1973, that abortion, under specific conditions, became the legal right of every female in the land. Prior to this date, forty-seven states virtually prohibited abortions, with

New York, Colorado, and Hawaii the only exceptions. (The new decision did not, however, make abortions legally available to all women, including minors, under all circumstances. The current status of abortion laws will be covered in greater detail further on in this chapter.)

The laws regulating sexual conduct cover a vast field. They often apply equally to minors and to adults. We shall concentrate on the questions that came up most often in interviews with your fellow students. Our sole purpose is to tell you what the law is—not to offer moral guidance or criticism. However, to clarify the reasoning behind the laws, we may quote directly from legal sources.

First, let's examine how the law in general looks at the marriage contract. In general, getting married is far easier than getting divorced. Once you are married you cannot revoke your marriage just by mutual agreement with your mate. You must submit to the dictates of the state:

> Marriage is a contract sui generis (in a class by itself), differing in notable respects from ordinary contracts . . . being usually accorded more dignity than the ordinary contract, and the rules applicable to ordinary contracts are not applied to marriage contracts because of the nature of the marriage relationship and for reasons of sound public policy. The chief difference from ordinary contracts is that the marriage contract cannot be revoked or dissolved by the parties, but only by the sovereign power of the state.

Likewise, the relationship cannot be changed by the parties whose rights and obligations depend, not on their agreement, but on statutory and common law.[1]

In other words, if you enter into a business partnership with someone, or a sales agreement, you can cancel the contract by mutual consent. The state need not be consulted. But when you enter into a marital contract, you cannot cancel it, even by mutual agreement. The legal status of this very personal relationship is in the hands of the state. This goes back to the time when marriage was considered a lifetime proposition, regulated by powerful canon law (church law).

When can minors marry without parental consent?

Regulations concerning marriage licenses are by statute. This means that they vary from state to state.

There are special regulations in some states which you should check before eloping to a state where the age requirements are lower. A few states, for example, require a waiting period of up to eight days to obtain a license. Others require a five-day wait after obtaining the license, before the marriage can take place. Furthermore, some regulations may have changed by the time you read this. Therefore, to be safe, it is best to check further.

The following table shows the legal requirements for marriage, state by state, as published in the *World Almanac, 1978.*

[1] *Corpus Juris Secundum,* Vol. 55, Paragraph 2, p. 809.

MARRIAGE INFORMATION

Source: Compiled by William E. Mariano, Council on Marriage Relations, Inc.,
110 E. 42d St., New York, NY 10017 (as of Oct. 1, 1977)

Marriageable age, by states, for both males and females with and without consent of parents or guardians. But in most states, the court has authority, in an emergency, to marry young couples below the ordinary age of consent, where due regard for their morals and welfare so requires. In many states, under special circumstances, blood test and waiting period may be waived.

State	With consent Men	With consent Women	Without consent Men	Without consent Women	Blood test Required	Blood test Other state accepted *	Wait for license	Wait after license
Alabama (b)	17	14	21	18	Yes	Yes	None	None
Alaska	18	16	19	18	Yes	No	3 days	None
Arizona	16 (i)	16	18	18	Yes	Yes	None	None
Arkansas	17	16 (j)	18	18	Yes	No	3 days	None
California	— (i)	— (i)	18	18	Yes	Yes	None	None
Colorado	16	16	18	18	Yes	—	None	None
Connecticut	16	16 (m)	18	18	Yes	Yes	4 days	None
Delaware	18	16 (j)	18	18	Yes	Yes	None	24 hrs. (c)
District of Columbia	18	16	21	18	Yes	Yes	3 days	None
Florida	18	16	21	21	Yes	Yes	3 days	None
Georgia	18	16	18	18	Yes	Yes	None (b)	None (k)
Hawaii	16	16	18	18	Yes	Yes	None	None
Idaho	16	16	18	18	Yes	Yes	None (i)	None
Illinois (a)	— (e)	15 (e)	18	18	Yes	Yes	None	None
Indiana	17	17	18	18	Yes	No	3 days	None
Iowa	16 (e)	16 (e)	18	18	Yes	Yes	3 days	None

MARRIAGE INFORMATION

State	With consent		Without consent		Blood test		Wait for license	Wait after license
	Men	Women	Men	Women	Required	Other state accepted *		
Kansas	(i)	— (i)	18	18	Yes	Yes	3 days	None
Kentucky	18	16	18	18	Yes	No	3 days	None
Louisiana (a)	18	16	18	18	Yes	No	None	72 hours
Maine	16	16	18	18	No	No	5 days	None
Maryland	18	16	21	18	None	None	48 hours	None
Massachusetts	— (i)	— (i)	18	18	Yes	Yes	3 days	None
Michigan (a)	—	16	18	18	Yes	No	3 days	None
Minnesota	—	16 (e)	18	18	None	—	5 days	None
Mississippi (b)	17	15	17	15	Yes	—	3 days	None
Missouri	15	15	18	18	Yes	Yes	3 days	None
Montana	— (i)	— (i)	18	18	Yes	Yes	5 days	None
Nebraska	18	16	18	18	Yes	Yes	5 days	None
Nevada	18	16	21	18	None	None	None	None
New Hampshire (a)	14 (e)	13 (e)	18	18	Yes	Yes	5 days	None
New Jersey (a)	—	16	18	18	Yes	Yes	72 hours	None
New Mexico	16	16	21	21	Yes	Yes	None	None
New York	16	14	18	18	Yes	No	None	24 hrs. (g)
North Carolina (a)	16	16	18	18	Yes	Yes	None	None
North Dakota (a)	— (i)	15	18	18	Yes	—	None	None
Ohio (a)	18	16	18	18	Yes	Yes	5 days	None
Oklahoma	16	16	18	18	Yes	No	None (f) (h)	—
Oregon	18 (e)	15 (e)	18	18	Yes	No	7 days	None
Pennsylvania	16	16	18	18	Yes	Yes	3 days	None

MARRIAGE INFORMATION

State	With consent Men	Women	Without consent Men	Women	Blood test Required	Other state accepted *	Wait for license	Wait after license
Rhode Island (a)(b)	18	16	18	18	Yes	No	None	None
South Carolina	16	14	18	18	None	None	24 hours	None
South Dakota	18	16	18	18	Yes	Yes	None	None
Tennessee (b)	16	16	21	21	Yes	Yes	3 days	None
Texas	16	16	18	18	Yes	Yes	None	None
Utah (a)	—(o)	—(o)	—(o)	—(o)	Yes	—	None	None
Vermont (a)	18	16	18	18	Yes	Yes (n)	None	5 days
Virginia (a)	16	16	18	18	Yes	—	None	None
Washington	17	17	18	18	(d)		3 days	None
West Virginia	(i)	16	18	18	Yes	No	3 days	None
Wisconsin	18	16	18	18	Yes	Yes	5 days	None
Wyoming	18	16	21	21	Yes	Yes	None	None
Puerto Rico	16	16	21	21	(f)	None	None	None
Virgin Islands	16	14	21	18	None	None	8 days	None

* Many states have additional special requirements; contact individual state. (a) Special laws applicable to non-residents. (b) Special laws applicable to those under 21 years; Ala., bond required if male is under 21, female under 18. (c) 24 hours if one or both parties resident of state; 96 hours if both parties are non-residents. (d) None, but male must file affidavit. (e) Parental consent plus court's consent required. (f) None, but a medical certificate is required. (g) Marriage may not be solemnized within 10 days from date of blood test. (h) If either under 21, 72 hrs. (i) Statute provides for obtaining license with parental or court consent with no state minimum age. (j) Under 16, with parental and court consent. (k) All those between 19–21 cannot waive 3 day waiting period. (l) If either under 18, wait 3 full days. (m) If under stated age, court consent required. (n) Va. blood test form must be used. (o) Ut. has recently amended its laws to eliminate distinctions of age based on sex. Current ages are not available.

If a teen-age couple, too young to marry in their own state, gets married out of state where the age limit for getting married without parental consent is lower, how valid is such a marriage?

As a general rule, the validity (or legality) of a marriage is determined by the law where the marriage took place. If a marriage is valid in the state where it took place, it is considered valid in other states. Therefore, the couple may return to their home state in the knowledge that they are legally married.

Is it ever possible for parents or guardians to invalidate (upset) an out-of-state marriage of minors?

First, let us quote directly from legal opinion:

An exception to the general rule [about the validity of marriages from state to state] is ordinarily made in the case of marriages repugnant to the public policy of the domicile of the parties, in respect of polygamy, incest, or miscegenation, *or otherwise contrary to its positive laws.*[2] (Italics ours.)

The italicized part of this legal opinion implies a lot of possible trouble. There are archaic statutes in many states concerning moral conduct. Though they are rarely used, they could be unearthed in an attempt to void a marriage.

Here is an illustration of how, in exception to the general rule, a marriage valid in the state where the

[2] *Ibid.,* Vol. 38, Paragraph 3, p. 1276.

couple was married, did not hold up in another state. A young doctor's uncle died. The doctor then married the widow, who was his aunt by marriage, not by blood relationship. In the state in which the couple married, this was perfectly legal. Then they moved to another state. Upon the doctor's death, the widow lost all claim to his estate because it was judged that their marriage was void to start with. Why? Because in the state to which they had moved, such a union was labeled incest. It violated a statute.

What about the reference to "miscegenation"? In law, this means marriage or cohabitation between a member of the white race and someone of another race. Laws prohibiting such marriages have been held to be unconstitutional and therefore invalid by the U.S. Supreme Court, so this pretext could not now be used to invalidate a marriage.

How does a common-law marriage relate to minors and how valid is it?

In a common-law marriage, a man and woman live together as husband and wife without a license or marriage ceremony—religious or civil. This practice is becoming more and more frequent among adults. Some banks even grant mortgage loans to couples who have been living together without benefit of marriage. However, there are only fourteen states that recognize common-law marriage as a legally binding relationship. They are: Alabama, Colorado, Georgia, Idaho, Iowa, Kansas, Montana, North Dakota, Oklahoma, Pennsylvania, Rhode Island, South Carolina,

Texas, and the District of Columbia. In all the other states a woman could not, for example, sue her common-law mate for support if he deserted her.

How does this specifically relate to younger couples—those who are still minors—who decide to live together openly and without benefit of marriage formalities? In the thirty-six states which do not recognize common-law marriage their relationship is not legally binding. Furthermore, they could be subject to legal penalties if someone, such as an angry parent, chose to cause trouble. On the other hand, in those fourteen states which do recognize common-law marriage they would find it very hard to separate —just as hard as if they had been married formally.

What restrictions are placed upon minors in obtaining legal abortions?

Minors have practically the same privileges as adults as a result of several U.S. Supreme Court decisions stemming from the 1973 decision in the case of *Jane Roe v. Henry Wade.* This decision held that a state cannot restrict a woman from terminating a pregnancy by abortion during the first trimester (the first twelve weeks of pregnancy) because to do so would violate the Due Process Clause of the Fourteenth Amendment of the Constitution. Some states, such as Missouri, challenged this ruling. The Missouri statute required written consent of parent or guardian to an abortion of an unmarried woman under eighteen, during her first twelve weeks of pregnancy, unless a licensed physician certified that an abortion was necessary to preserve the mother's life. However, a 1976 Supreme Court decision stated that the Missouri statute was unconstitutional. As a result of this and other decisions a woman (minor or adult) has the legal right in every state to obtain an abortion during the first twelve weeks of her pregnancy. Here is how this liberalization of the abortion laws came about and what it entails as it now stands:

An unmarried pregnant woman in Texas, who wished to have an abortion, brought suit in the U.S. District Court to the effect that the Texas criminal abortion statutes were unconstitutional as they stood. She sought an injunction against their continued enforcement.

The three-judge District Court held, among other things, that the right to choose whether to have children was protected by the Ninth through the Fourteenth Amendments and that the Texas criminal abortion statutes were void because they were unconstitutionally vague and broad in scope. However, the court still denied her the right to go ahead and have the abortion in defiance of the Texas statutes.

As a result, the case was appealed to the U.S. Supreme Court, which held as follows:

(1) She had the right to sue.

(2) The right to privacy "encompasses a woman's decision whether or not to terminate her pregnancy."

(3) States do have legitimate interests in seeing to it that abortions are performed under conditions that ensure maximum safety for the patient.

(4) A woman's right to terminate her pregnancy

may, to some extent, be modified by the state's legitimate interests in protecting her health, in maintaining proper medical standards, and in protecting potential human life.

(5) However, "prior to the end of the first trimester of pregnancy, the state may not interfere or regulate an attending physician's decision, reached in consultation with his patient, that the patient's pregnancy should be terminated."

(6) After that and until such time as the fetus becomes viable (which means that it has attained sufficient development to be capable of living outside the uterus), the state may regulate abortion procedure only to the extent that such regulation relates to the protection of the mother's health.

(7) When the fetus becomes viable, the state may prohibit abortions altogether, except those necessary to preserve the life or health of the mother.[3]

From this somewhat abbreviated description of this momentous decision, you can see that a female, regardless of age, is legally entitled to have a physician perform an abortion, without any question, during the first twelve weeks of pregnancy. If a minor encounters resistance, or has questions, her best procedure is to contact the nearest Planned Parenthood office. They can refer her to a clinic to have an abortion—and they will first consult with her personally.

What legal penalties does a male minor risk if he has sexual intercourse with a female minor?

[3] This data is from: *U.S. Supreme Court Reports*, Lawyer's Edition, Vol. 35 L, Ed 2d #1, Feb. 15, 1973, pp. 1–281.

Under certain circumstances, he runs the risk of being accused of "statutory rape" if either the girl or her parents wish to bring up the matter in a court of law. A male minor can be so accused, under most statutes, if he is over fourteen. If he is younger, he is considered incapable of such an act.

Specifically, statutory rape is "carnal knowledge" (a legal euphemism for sexual intercourse) of a female child under a specified age, either with or without her consent. Carnal knowledge of a female with her consent is not rape if she is above the age specified by statute. This specified age is called the "age of consent." It differs from state to state.

> . . . The purpose of these statutes is to protect young females from illicit acts of the opposite sex by rendering such females under the specified age incapable of consenting to sexual intercourse. Thus sexual intercourse with a female under the age of consent at common law or as fixed by statute constitutes rape or the statutory crime of carnal knowledge, whether or not the act be accomplished against her will, or with or without her consent. It makes no difference whether or not the female has passed the age of puberty; if she is under the age limit fixed by statute, consent is immaterial and all sexual intercourse is rape.
>
> . . . A female under the specified age does not by marriage become capable of consenting to illicit sexual intercourse, and, in a prosecution for rape or carnal knowledge of a female under the age of consent, it is immaterial whether she had been married.[4]

4 *Corpus Juris Secundum*, Vol. 75, Paragraph 13, p. 479.

If a teen-age boy impregnates a girl who is below the age of consent, the girl or her parents could bring charges against him. The punishment for statutory rape is imprisonment.

What risks does a minor couple take if they live together openly?

The charge of criminal "fornication" could be brought against such a couple (minor or adult) in those states where such a statute still exists. What does this involve and how did such a law come about?

> Fornication was punishable in England by the ecclesiastical courts as an ecclesiastical offense; but it was not recognized or punished as a crime at common law unless committed openly and notoriously so as to constitute a public nuisance; it was not punished simply as fornication. The rule prevailing in the United States is that at common law and in absence of statutory change mere fornication is not a criminal offense, and becomes an offense only in cases of open lewdness amounting to nuisance.[5]
>
> While a single, clandestine act of sexual intercourse constitutes fornication in the usual acceptance of the word, habitual acts of intercourse over a period of time may be necessary to the offense of fornication as defined by statute. Under a statute providing that whenever a man and a single woman "cohabit" with each other both shall be guilty of fornication, it is essential to commission of the offense that the parties dwell together for some period of time and make a practice of sexual intercourse while so dwelling, but

[5] *Corpus Juris Secundum,* Vol. 37, Paragraph 2, p. 119.

it is not necessary that they dwell together as husband and wife or that their intercourse be open and notorious. Under statutes requiring that the parties shall cohabit in a state of fornication to constitute the offense, they must live together in the manner of husband and wife for some period of time in order to commit fornication, and single or occasional meetings for illicit intercourse are not an offense under the statute.[6]

This means essentially that a single act or two is seldom interpreted as fornication in the legal sense, but acts committed over a period of time may be. In some states, if the word "cohabit" is used alone, any such relationship maintained over a period of time will be regarded as fornication. However, if the words "cohabit in a state of fornication" are used the unmarried couple must live together as husband and wife for the relationship to be considered fornication.

So, as we so often find, the laws about fornication vary from state to state.

Punishment for fornication is by fine or imprisonment or both. (If it is considered a misdemeanor under statute, the punishment is generally left up to the judge.) Thus, it is possible for parents or anyone else to have you charged with fornication if you live together where there are statutes against it.

Do minors have the right to engage in a homosexual relationship?

[6] *Ibid.,* Paragraph 4, p. 121.

Laws about homosexuality are generally the same for minors as for adults. Despite the fact that there is growing enlightenment regarding homosexual behavior, despite the recognition by most psychiatrists that homosexuality is not a "sickness," legal reference books continue to refer to it as "sodomy," or as "an unnatural act," or as "an act against nature." Many so-called modern statutes define sodomy as an act "committed either by the anus or by or with the mouth, or in any opening of the body except sexual parts." [7] And sodomy, whether committed by persons of the opposite or same sex, may be punishable by fine or imprisonment, or both. However, prosecution today is seldom carried out. In earlier times, under common law, sodomy was punishable by death—usually by burning or by burying alive.

The law links homosexuality to sodomy as follows:

Sexual acts between men have generally been understood to come within the offense of sodomy. However, it has also been held that copulation per os between two women constitutes sodomy inasmuch as the word "mankind" in a statute making it an offense to commit the crime against nature with mankind includes both male and female. But it has been also held that the crime of sodomy proper cannot be accomplished between two women under a statute defining sodomy as the carnal knowledge and connection against the

[7] American Jurisprudence Second, Vol. 70, Paragraph 7, p. 811.

order of nature, by men with men, or in the same unnatural manner with women. And a statute making it an offense for one to take into his or her mouth the sexual organ of any person, or to place his or her sexual organ in the mouth of any other person, has been held not to apply to lesbian activity.[8]

This means that, while lesbian activity is seldom classed as sodomy, a homosexual relationship between males is so classed. Technically sodomy is a punishable offense. Nowadays, however, there is growing opposition to enforcement of these laws.

Can minors legally get birth control information and contraceptives?

Yes. The Planned Parenthood League will provide contraceptive advice and supplies to minors. Your nearest Planned Parenthood League will give you up-to-date information.

Can minors be treated for VD without parental consent?

More and more states are permitting confidential treatment for venereal disease. Consult the Planned Parenthood League for the regulations in your state, and for information on the location of VD clinics.

In view of the Supreme Court's decisions on abortion, how easy is it for a minor to obtain an abortion legally?

We have already stated that the Supreme Court seems to have cleared the way for a minor to get an

[8] *Ibid.*

abortion without her parent's permission (see page 44). (This, of course, applies just to an abortion performed in the first three months of pregnancy, by a doctor.) As of this writing, however, there is a move afoot to introduce a constitutional amendment which would prohibit abortions despite the 1973 Supreme Court decision. Furthermore, some areas in the country still try to obstruct the rights of both minors and adults to have abortions. If you meet with difficulty, you should consult the nearest Planned Parenthood League office.

CHAPTER FOUR

Minors for Hire—Working Rights and Restrictions

In our opening chapter, we pointed out that the laws about jobs for minors were originally meant to protect you. If parts of the common law and some statutes strike you as unfair, remember that only a little over one generation ago children were "allowed" to work in factories and farms, often at the expense of their education and health.

What are the job limitations a minor faces?

These standards are set forth by the federal Fair Labor Standards Act:

> The Fair Labor Standards Act provides that no employer may employ any "oppressive child labor" in commerce or in the production of goods for commerce, or in any enterprise engaged in commerce or in the production of goods for commerce. Further, the act prohibits the shipment in commerce of goods produced in establishments where such labor has been employed.
>
> The child labor provisions of the Fair Labor Standards Act are not limited in operation to situations where child labor has a harmful effect on the maintenance of the minimum wage rate; they apply regardless of any effect upon the wage structure.[1]

[1] *American Jurisprudence Second,* Vol. 48, Paragraph 1677, p. 1037.

This is tough wording. If the government thinks any occupation might be harmful to minors, it is termed "oppressive child labor"—with no exceptions.

Here is a list of occupations which are expressly forbidden for those under eighteen years of age:

Manufacturing and storing of explosives

Driving a motor vehicle or acting as outside helper

Coal mining

Logging and sawmill activities

Power-driven woodworking

Activities exposing workers to radioactive substances

Operation of power-driven hoisting apparatus

Operation of power-driven metal-forming machines

Mining other than coal mining

Operation of bakery machines

Slaughtering and meatpacking

Operation of paper-products machines

Manufacturing of brick and tile

Operation of power-driven saws and shears

Wrecking and demolition

Roofing

Excavation and certain activities in agriculture.[2]

In addition to federal regulations, there are statutes in each state which are meant as protection.

[2] *Ibid.*, Vol. 48, Paragraph 1678, p. 1038.

What protection do minors have in regard to hours of work?

They have the same protection as adults—a forty-hour week.

Are minors entitled to overtime pay?

The word "overtime" is of variable meaning under the provisions of the Fair Labor Standards Act. Sometimes it is used to denote work after regular hours; sometimes work beyond hours prescribed by contract which are less than the statutory maximum number of hours; and sometimes hours outside of a specific clock pattern without regard to whether previous work has been done, as, for example, work on a Sunday or holiday.[3]

An employee is an employee whether minor or adult, and the same rules apply to both. Any work time over forty hours a week is overtime. However, if you work forty hours but there is a union contract that work beyond thirty-five hours is overtime, you would be entitled to time and a half for five hours' work. On the other hand, if you work thirty-five hours a week and there is no such union contract, you could be required to work the additional five hours without overtime pay. Before making a claim for overtime, be sure you know the specific regulations where you work. You can also check the Labor Department in your state.

[3] *Ibid.,* Paragraph 1550, p. 962.

Do minors have vacation time protection?

There is no law giving the right to vacations. Vacations vary from firm to firm, but minors have the same vacation privileges as adults.

Does the minimum wage law apply to minors?

Generally speaking, yes. As of 1977, under the Fair Labor Standards Act, the wage rates were set at a minimum of $2.65 an hour for all occupations, including agriculture.

Some minimum wage laws don't apply to jobs which are casual or at irregular intervals; however, they do apply if the job is part-time but on a regular basis, such as three times a week.

When can or must minors join a labor union?

Here, minors are subject to the same rules as adults. If you work in an all-union shop, you must usually join the union to get a job.

Must an employer take out withholding taxes and social security from a minor's pay?

Yes, just as in the case of an adult's paycheck.

Can minors claim their parents as dependents?

Only if they live with their parents and contribute 50 percent or more to their parents' support; or if the parents have less than $675 a year in income.

Should minors file a tax return?

No matter how small your annual wages, if they have been subject to withholding you should file. You may be entitled to a refund. If you earned $2,950 (the minimum in effect in 1978) or more, you *must* file a tax return.

CHAPTER FIVE

School Authority and Student Rights

It is not surprising that the students we interviewed had so many questions concerning school. If nursery school and kindergarten are included, a minor spends about fourteen years in school. And the school's power often seems as great as a parent's. It is important to understand how, why, and by whom this authority has been delegated to the schools.

In general, schools are not much affected by federal or state laws. Their policies are determined chiefly by local school boards which have the power to make rules and regulations to control the pupils. Even so, a school board does not have the right to deny a student his or her constitutional rights. As a result, there have been many issues which have been challenged in the courts by individual students and parents. In many cases the courts have been reactionary in their decisions, and in some very important cases such decisions have been overturned by the Supreme Court.

For example, here is how a law book described segregated schooling twenty-five years ago:

Where separate schools for white and colored children have been required or established by constitution or statute, the right to be admitted is restricted, each to the school of his race, provided the advantages and facilities furnished for both races are equal. Admission of a colored child to a white school can be required only on a showing that equality of treatment is not obtainable in separate schools, and in some jurisdictions, under statutes expressly declaring that separate schools shall be maintained for white and colored children, a colored child cannot be admitted to a white school even though there is no colored school in the district, the court intimating that the proper remedy is an action to compel the directors to establish a colored school.[1]

When this was written in 1952, there were still eighteen states which had segregated schooling. It was not until 1954 that the Supreme Court declared segregated schooling unconstitutional, leaving the problem of how to desegregate school systems largely unresolved to this day.

As a general rule, the courts shy away from interfering in school policies. They are not interested in the reasons, good or bad, for a school's regulations. Usually, the courts will intervene only if they believe that the school has exceeded its legal powers. In many ways, then, each local school board is like a dictatorship because it is comparatively free from federal or state regulations. However, school regulations are pretty similar throughout the country. Our replies to specific questions describe the average policy today in American school systems.

[1] *Corpus Juris Secundum,* Vol. 79, Paragraph 447, p. 353.

Can students attend a public school different from the one to which they have been assigned?

As a general rule, the answer is "No." There are exceptions, but they are few. For example, you might be able to transfer if your present school doesn't have certain courses that you need. Or you might be able to transfer to a closer school if you've been assigned to one that is far from your home. But, as the law states, ". . . convenience . . . may depend on considerations other than distance from the pupil's home." [2]

In addition, "the neighborhood school concept has been newly challenged where such assignment of pupils may result in racially imbalanced schools. . . . A board is precluded from 'gerrymandering' school attendance lines so as to consciously segregate pupils on the basis of race alone." [3]

This means that you could apply to transfer from a school that is racially segregated. If, however, the school board denied your request, the only other step would be to sue. "Some courts have ruled that a school board has an affirmative duty to correct racial imbalance where such imbalance is 'too great.' " [4]

What freedom do students have to reject "required" subjects?

[2] *Ibid.*, Paragraph 451, p. 353.
[3] *Ibid.*, pp. 152–153.
[4] *Ibid.*, p. 153.

Generally, the state has the power to choose the curriculum. Otherwise, the school board chooses it. In either case, students have to take the curriculum required by the school. In other words, you have no choice.

Can minors be barred from school because they get married?

Usually not:

> [The] rule requiring students who marry to withdraw from school has been considered by most courts to be unreasonable . . . the state guarantees free public education as a right to those of school age, and marriage alone does not nullify such a guarantee.[5]

However, not every school will abide by this. Unless there is a specific law that married students may attend school, the school board may refuse to allow it. (On the other hand, if you marry, you are not required to attend school.)

Can a minor be barred from school because she is pregnant?

She may be barred from school in some places, but not everywhere. The reason for barring a pregnant girl is usually that she "disrupts" the school. However, she may return to school after her pregnancy. Some school systems have special classes for pregnant girls. The rules may also differ from

[5] M. C. Nolte, *Guide to School Law* (West Nyack, N.Y.: Parker Publishing Co., 1969).

state to state according to whether the minor is married or unmarried.

What about an unmarried student father?

So far, there is no legal precedent for barring him.

What can students do about a teacher they believe is incompetent?

Not much. Generally, the school board has the power to dismiss a teacher for "justifiable cause." This may be defined by statute; if it is not, the school board can make its own rules concerning justifiable cause. Among the usual causes are: insubordination or violation of rules and regulations of the school board, lack of cooperation, incompetence, lack of efficiency in teaching and discipline, willful and persistent negligence, engaging in subversive activities, or conviction of a crime.

If a student, or a group of students, feels that a teacher is incompetent, the first step would be to convince the principal who, in turn, would have to convince the school board to remove the teacher. Obviously, this doesn't happen very often.

What rights do teachers have to discipline students, and what protection do students have against discipline?

First, here is how the law regards the role of the teacher:

As a general rule a school teacher, to a limited extent at least, stands *in loco parentis* [in place of the parent] to pupils under his charge, and may exercise such powers of control, restraint, and correction over them as may be reasonably necessary to enable him properly to perform his duties as teacher and accomplish the purpose of education. . . .

If nothing unreasonable is demanded, he has the right to direct how and when each pupil shall attend to his appropriate duties, and the manner in which a pupil shall demean himself. The control of the pupil exists during school hours, and even at a meeting of the student body of the school where it is held during school hours in the assembly hall of the school. The teacher's power and duty extend beyond the teaching and preservation of order and discipline to matters affecting morals, health, and safety of his pupils, and he may and should do everything he deems necessary to these ends, when they are not in conflict with the primary purposes of the school or opposed to law or rule of the school board. . . . [6]

Thus, because a teacher is considered as being "in the place of the parent," he has broad implied powers. However, there are limitations. These are worth quoting because the language shows the spirit of the law and also how vague the law can be.

The enforcement of a school rule or regulation must be reasonable under all the circumstances; and in such enforcement due regard must be had to the health, comfort, age, and mental and physical condition of the pupil and to the circumstances attending

[6] *Corpus Juris Secundum,* Vol. 79, Paragraph 493, p. 442.

each particular emergency; and the condition of weather, the infirmity of the pupil, and the like may require relaxation in a strict enforcement.[7]

As a general rule, a teacher is authorized to take measures such as removing a pupil from the room, disarming him, or detaining him after school hours, and to inflict such humane and reasonable punishment as he may deem most conducive to the enforcement of the rules and regulations of the school board and the good discipline and order of the school, and even for misconduct in respect of which no formal rules have been prescribed, but authority to go beyond this limit is not given a teacher by a school board's request that he be more strict than his predecessor in compelling obedience to rule.

A teacher has no right to inflict cruel and unusual punishment, to search children on suspicion or to exercise by virtue of his office discretionary quasi-judicial powers. The punishment must be for some specific offense and not excessive. There must be reasonable ground for the offense and no malice.[8]

An interesting fact is that all these conditions and actions are based on specific court cases resulting from students bringing suit against a school for unjust or cruel treatment. If you do object to the way a teacher has treated you, your first step is to make a complaint, either on your own, or with your parents, to the school authorities; if necessary to the school board. If that fails, all you can do is to sue—which can be time-consuming, and costs a great deal.

[7] *Ibid.*
[8] *Corpus Juris Secundum,* Vol. 79, Paragraph 501, p. 447.

Do teachers have the right to inflict physical punishment?

The answer is yes. Although many states have laws against physical punishment, in April, 1977, the U.S. Supreme Court rendered a decision (Ingraham v. Wright, #75-6527, 45 US LW4364) which seems to make those laws invalid:

Corporal punishment as administered by public school teachers to discipline recalcitrant students is not cruel and unusual punishment. The prohibition against cruel and unusual punishment under the Eighth Amendment was designed to protect those convicted of crime and thus does not extend to public school disciplinary practices.

Also, the due process clause of the Fourteenth Amendment does not require notice and hearing prior to imposition of corporal punishment as that practice is authorized and limited by the common law. The Florida statutory scheme, in view of the openness of the school environment, affords significant protection against unjustified corporal punishment of school children. Not only must the teacher and principal exercise prudence and restraint but also if the punishment is later found to be excessive, criminal penalties may be imposed upon the teacher and the principal.

To impose additional administrative safeguards as a constitutional requirement would require an unjustified diversion of school funds and would intrude into the area of educational responsibility that primarily lies with public school authorities.[9]

9 *U.S. Supreme Court Bulletin,* Vol. 37, No. 36, April 19, 1977.

For what reasons can students be suspended or dismissed from school?

Here are some of the grounds for expulsion or suspension which have been upheld by court decision in the past.

Continued absence without satisfactory excuses

Refusal to obey proper orders or regulations

Refusal to write a composition

Refusal to obey when told to read from a book prescribed by the school committee

Failure to come to school with a required exercise worked out, or with a reasonable excuse for not having done it

Refusal to present a certificate from a physician as to condition after a throat infection, or to submit to examination by the school physician on the ground of conscientious objections as a Christian Scientist

Refusal to give the name of a pupil who has been guilty of a breach of the rules

Making a speech in a school meeting criticizing the school board

Publishing in a local newspaper a satirical poem reflecting on the regulations of the school

Being drunk or disorderly "on Christmas Day on the village streets in violation of the village ordinance"

Being unable to maintain a satisfactory rate of progress with other students at a normal school (if there is such a statute)

When can students stop going to school?

There is no federal law regulating this. However, over 50 percent of U.S. school districts have laws that say you must attend school from age seven to age sixteen. In some states, level of education rather than age determines when one can leave school.

Does the school have the right to search students' lockers?

Technically, no. Searching students' lockers is an infringement of their constitutional rights under the Fourth Amendment. But in fact, constitutional rights are sometimes disregarded, and the law here is still undefined:

> It is not clear whether student lockers are areas protected from search or whether they constitute leased "quarters" which still belong to the school, but which are temporarily utilized for the convenience of the student.[10]

This legal guide goes on to refer to bomb scares which would seem to justify a search for the safety of the students. But searches for drugs, weapons, pornography, and such are not mentioned. It is quite common for schools to search students' lockers and, until someone sues, this practice will continue.

Does the school have the right to prohibit the passing out of leaflets by the students?

If a school considers the leaflets to be subver-

[10] M. C. Nolte, *Guide to School Law* (West Nyack, N.Y.: Parker Publishing Co., 1969), p. 114.

sive and disruptive to school discipline, it can prohibit their distribution. (The students can protest this ruling through court action since they are supposed to enjoy the same protection of the First Amendment inside the school grounds as adults do outside it. A specific case involving a similar matter is described further on.)

Does the school have the right to prevent a speaker, chosen by the students, from speaking on school property?

Yes. On the same grounds as above.

Do the police have a right to examine students' school records?

Yes. However, no other outsider is allowed to do so because these records are considered confidential.

Do students have the right to see their own records?

Yes, they do. In November of 1974 Congress amended the Freedom of Information Act to insure this right. You or your parents have the right to see your official school records.

Can students be subjected to disciplinary actions by the school for acts they have committed outside school and after school hours?

Although a schoolteacher or a school board ordinarily has no right of control over a child after he has returned to his home or his parents' control and cannot punish him for ordinary acts of misbehavior thereafter, the supervision and control of a teacher over a pupil, and of a school board to make needful rules for the conduct of the pupils, are not confined to the schoolroom and school premises, but extend over the pupil from the time he leaves home to go to school until he returns home from school, and, where the effect of acts done out of a schoolroom, while the pupils are coming to or going from school, reaches within the schoolroom and is detrimental to good order and the best interests of the school, such acts may be forbidden and the teacher may punish an offending pupil when he comes to school, but the connection between the prohibited acts and the discipline and welfare of the school must be direct and immediate, not remote and indirect.[11]

There are conflicting opinions as to how far the school may regulate students' conduct. Some legal opinion holds that a school may punish students for acts committed after they have returned to their homes if the acts are harmful to school discipline; for example, holding a teacher up to ridicule. But others say that school boards do not have this authority. Students may protest such discipline by court action and must then rely on the opinion of the court, or they may appeal to a higher court.

Does the school have the right to prohibit certain types of wearing apparel and hair styles?

Yes. There are few, if any, statutes about dress. This matter is left up to the individual school and

---

[11] *Corpus Juris Secundum*, Vol. 79, Paragraph 496, p. 445.

school board. They do have the right to regulate dress and hair style. As a rule, they go along with current styles and fads, but they do not have to. Only successful individual court action could overturn such a restriction on a student.

Do students have the right to wear buttons or arm bands to advertise or protest political action?

Students—in theory—have this right as long as such activities do not disrupt the peaceful operation of the school. But the phrase "operation of the school" offers a lot of leeway. Here is a case in point.

A school board in Des Moines, learned that some students were going to wear black arm bands to protest the Vietnam War. The board passed a resolution to prohibit this action on the school's property. The students, in turn, brought suit. The question was whether the school officials were depriving the students of their constitutional rights under the First Amendment. The decision went against the students. The lower court in 1966 held that "School officials must be given wide discretion . . . [in dealing with distractions] and if, under the circumstances, a disturbance in school discipline is reasonably to be anticipated, actions which are reasonably calculated to prevent such a disruption must be upheld by the Court. In the case now before the Court, the regulation of the defendant school district was, under the circumstances, reasonable and did not deprive the plaintiffs of their Constitutional right to freedom of speech."

Three years later, in 1969, the U.S. Supreme Court reversed this decision. Several things should be noted in this example. First, because of the school board's action, the students were prevented from wearing the arm bands. Second, although the students felt they were in the right they lost the case in the lower court. That is, you can sue, but you may lose—and if you win, your victory may not be immediate. You should also be aware that even Supreme Court decisions are sometimes simply ignored. To press for enforcement of the law may take time and money. (For example, this is often the case in questions of abortion, as we have seen.)

CHAPTER SIX

Parents of Minors— Obligations, Rights, and Restrictions

In our interviews, students were just as interested in their parents' legal authority as in the authority of schools.

First, here is the background of parental rights. Minors are in a bind when it comes to their relationship to their parents. On the one hand, they want to be independent, to operate more or less as they choose. On the other hand, they depend upon their parents for financial support and protection. Parents, in turn, have no choice, but are obliged by law to support, educate, and control their children, until the children reach at least age sixteen, or in some states, the age of majority.

Under some circumstances, if a minor is mentally or physically handicapped at the age of majority, the parent must continue to support him or her. You can see, therefore, that the parent-child relationship is a two-sided problem. Just as there are young people in their teens who would like to have complete independence, so there are some parents who would like to get out from under their obligations of parenthood. The purpose of the law is to try to establish rules for parent and child to live by with a minimum of conflict.

Here is a general, legal definition of the parent-child relationship:

The relation of parent and child is a status, and not a property right. The existence of the relation of parent and child is generally a question of fact, to be determined by the facts and circumstances of the particular case, and is established prima facie (based on immediate impression) where it is shown that the parties lived together and recognized by their acts the existence of that relation. Where there is a living parent the presumption prevails that the relationship of parent and child continues to exist, and it cannot be loosely destroyed or abandoned by the parent through agreement or otherwise, since it is against public policy to destroy or even limit the relation of parent and child except for adequate legal reasons.[1]

This means that the main thrust of the law is to protect the child from being abandoned by a parent. Therefore, it is not surprising that children, who benefit from support and protection, are also subject to obligations and restrictions.

While the courts may try to be understanding to both parent and child, they usually tip the scales in favor of the parents. For example, the United States Supreme Court, in a decision rendered in June of 1977, ruled that a foster child may ordinarily be moved away from its foster family without a hearing. The Justices upheld New York State regulations that require a hearing only if the foster family requests it and has been caring for the child for at least eighteen months. They said that under state law a natural parent has a right in most instances to the return of a child voluntarily placed in foster care.

[1] *Corpus Juris Secundum*, Vol. 67, Paragraph 3, p. 628.

In other words, the child's wishes here have no bearing on the natural parents' right to reclaim him or her from foster parents. And remember that a child is legally defined as anyone below the age of eighteen.

Before we proceed to specifics, one further point should be understood. It is actually at the heart of the entire subject—how the law looks upon the authority of the parent:

> By the common law, parental rights, like most rights pertaining to the family, were vested in the father alone. During his life the mother, at least under ordinary circumstances, had no parental rights recognized by law. She was entitled, it was said, "only to reverence and respect." The modern tendency, however, is toward the equalization of the rights of the father and mother. This is evidenced by the adoption of statutes in many jurisdictions making the father and mother joint guardians over their children, or expressly providing that the father and mother shall have the joint and equal right to the custody, control, and services of the child. A transfer of the parental status and rights from the father to the mother may be made by agreement, tacit or express, between them.

> If the child is illegitimate, the mother is the sole legal parent, and all the rights of parenthood are vested in her, although, on her death, the father's rights are generally recognized as superior to those of third persons.

> On the death of the father, it is generally held that the widowed mother becomes the legal parent of the

minor children, with substantially the same right which the father had during his lifetime. However, a seventeenth century British statute, which became part of our common law, provided for the father to designate a testamentary guardian who would have rights paramount to those of the mother. Though testamentary guardianship is recognized in most of our states, it has been modified by statute in many to give the mother more favorable treatment.

If a man abandons his wife and children, he is held to have forfeited his rights, or transferred them to the mother, in whose care the children remain. The widowed or abandoned mother becomes, therefore, the natural guardian of her children, with substantially the same rights previously held by the father.

The relative rights of the father and mother may be fixed by a decree of court, either in proceedings directly concerning the custody of the child or in divorce proceedings between the parents. Where this is the case, of course, general principles become subordinate to the terms of the decree. However, where there is no question as to custody, the courts will not undertake to resolve a conflict between maternal and paternal authority.[2]

This quotation establishes that, nowadays, mother and father share custody and control over a child. Now let's see what the word "control" encompasses. Here is how another legal reference book defines it:

[2] *American Jurisprudence Second,* Vol. 59, Paragraphs 11–12, pp. 94–95.

Parents have the authority, and it is their legal, as well as their natural, duty to care for, control, and protect their minor children, and, where a parent asserts his right to the custody of a child, he must also assume all duties in connection therewith, and, moreover, the law recognizes no distinction of color or race in the parental relation, but all parents, whatever may be their standing in society, have precisely the same legal authority and control over their children. In the exercise of such authority and duty a parent may exercise a wide discretion, but he must not so act as to endanger the child's safety or morals, nor, in some states, may he enter into a contract with a third person which releases him from such duties. A father has the right to forbid a prospective suitor, of whom he does not approve, to call on his daughter.[3]

There are several important points here which should be noted.

First, the authority of parents is almost absolute: parents have wide discretion; how they exert their authority is limited only by their not being allowed to endanger their children's safety or impair their morals.

Second, emphasis is placed on the fact that parents must support as well as control their children.

Third, a father may regulate the kinds of people his minor child associates with, and may bar a daughter's boyfriend from the house.

Parents also have the right to determine the type

---

[3] *Corpus Juris Secundum,* Vol. 67, Paragraph 6, p. 630.

of education for their children and the occupation children may have while under the parents' control. This gives parents almost complete legal control over the children's activities.

Can a parent, or parents, give adult status to a minor, with all the responsibilities and privileges which go with it?

Giving minors adult status is called *emancipation.* Under certain circumstances, parents can voluntarily emancipate minors if the parents renounce all legal duties and surrender all legal rights as parents. This does not mean, however, that if minors live away from home they are automatically emancipated. Nor are they emancipated when they are allowed to keep all their earnings from a job. The parent has to say or write or imply the *intention* to emancipate the child.

Here is when and how emancipation usually occurs: when minors have a business of their own and are in full charge of it, or when minors work for others and keep all their wages and are allowed to spend their money as they please. However, only under exceptional circumstances can minors emancipate themselves. Ordinarily only their parents can do this. If minors leave home, they are not emancipated as long as the parent has not consented to it. Conversely, minors can be emancipated even though they do live at home.

There are some situations where minors can be considered emancipated even if their parents make no such declaration or implication. One of these is when a father who is financially able to support his minor son forces him to leave home and get a job elsewhere for his own keep. Another is if a minor is deserted or abandoned by his parents. Either of these illegal acts on the part of parents automatically emancipate the minor.

What duties and obligations does a father have toward his children?

By law, though not always in fact, a father cannot simply wash his hands of responsibility toward a minor. He may not either abandon or emancipate a minor against his or her will in order to avoid supporting the child. He must support and educate his children. This is required. Any decree to the contrary (say, a divorce decree) is null and void. Moreover, father support is regarded as a "principle of natural law."

Neither poverty nor unwillingness to work relieves a father of this obligation. Furthermore, a child's needs are in relation to a father's ability to pay for them. This is important because it means that a father who is well-off cannot dress his children in rags, or feed them food which is inferior, or deprive them of medical care which he can well afford to provide.

This does not mean, however, that a minor can go to the local court and file a claim against his or her father. In order to protest effectively, children should go to a clergyman, or a doctor, or a family agency, or some trusted adult. If the adult they appeal to feels their complaints are valid, the adult would then place the matter in a lawyer's hands.

Are parents allowed to use corporal (physical) punishment and what, if anything, can minors do to protest against it?

A parent, being charged with the training and education of his child, has the right to exercise such control and restraint and to adopt such disciplinary measures for the child as will enable him to discharge his parental duty. Accordingly, he has the right to correct the child by reasonable and timely punishment, including corporal punishment. And the child has no right to resist such punishment by the parent unless the amount of force used or the means employed is such as to render such punishment abusive rather than corrective. A parent has a wide discretion in the performance of such functions. The control and proper discipline of a child by the parent may justify acts which would otherwise constitute assault and battery or false imprisonment.

The right of chastisement is founded on the welfare of the child, not on the parent's liberty of action. Accordingly, the right of parental discipline clearly has its limits. And if the limits are exceeded, the parent may be criminally liable for assault or other offenses, or even, if death results, for murder or manslaughter. He may also, if the jurisdiction is one in which a minor child is allowed to sue his parent for a wilful tort, be civilly liable for assault and battery. The courts, however, are not in full agreement as to how the limits are defined.

The rule recognized by a majority of the courts is that a parent may, without criminal liability, inflict such punishment as is reasonable under the facts and circumstances. Under this view, no general rule as to what is permissible can be laid down, since the amount of force which would be reasonable or excessive must vary with the age, sex, physical condition, and other characteristics of the child and with the gravity of the offense for which he is being punished. And the reasonableness or excessiveness of the punishment, under all the circumstances, is a question for the jury. Some courts, however, take the view that a parent, in punishing a child, acts in a judicial or quasi-judicial capacity, and is not criminally liable for an error in judgment, or because the fact-finder thinks the punishment disproportionate to the misconduct, but is liable only if the punishment resulted in permanent injury or death, or was inflicted with malice, express or implied. Under either view, where punishment is inflicted with malice or causes permanent injury or death, the parental privilege is exceeded and the parent will be criminally liable, unless special statutory provisions require a contrary result.

The right of punishment extends to persons in loco parentis. The parent may delegate the right of punishment to another, but, of course, such substituted or delegated right is subject to the same limits of moderation and reasonableness as in the case of the parent.[4]

Two important points are covered in this quota-

---

[4] *American Jurisprudence Second,* Vol. 59, Paragraphs 24–25, pp. 106–107.

tion. First, no age limit is set as to when parents may administer corporal punishment to minor children. Whether the children are four or fourteen, it appears to be the parents' right to use corporal punishment. And second, the vagueness of the terms "excessive, immoderate and unreasonable" gives parents a good deal of leeway as to how severely they can punish their children.

Where does the law draw the line between reasonable and excessive punishment and how effectively does it prevent the latter?

The law continues to lean over backward to give parents a good deal of leeway. Furthermore, efforts to prevent child abuse remain frighteningly ineffectual. Although, today, the American public is more aware of the horrors of child abuse, the issue takes a back seat compared to, say, the "energy crisis" which affects immediate adult comfort and convenience. Worse yet, experts in the field of child abuse state that for every case reported probably one hundred more take place. However, in many areas there is now a way for minors or adults to report cases of child abuse. Look for *Child Abuse Careline* in your telephone book. It is a toll-free number in operation twenty-four hours a day. Anyone may call to report cases of abuse, and each report is confidential and will be investigated. If there is no listing for this service in your area, you can call the hospital or the police department. If you are reluctant to do this yourself, ask a reliable adult to make the call for you.

The following case history illustrates the child abuse situation poignantly and to the point. It is quoted from Dr. Vincent J. Fontana's book *Somewhere a Child Is Crying.*

Connie hadn't even been born when a county domestic-relations court took her ten-month-old sister, Bettina, away from the natural mother, Mrs. Sally Colby, after a finding of neglect. Bettina had infected injuries about her eyes and ears. Emergency room doctors felt she might have been abused, but they had no proof. It was hard to believe that young Mrs. Colby, a lonely divorcee who appeared to be terribly anxious about Bettina, could have deliberately hurt her child. Neglected her, perhaps, while she was trying to earn a living but hurt her, no. Nevertheless, Bettina was placed with foster parents.

A few months later, Sally Colby became Mrs. Lewis Erhard and settled down with her new husband in a modest, but comfortable, ranch-style house. They were very happy when Connie was born. Neighbors saw them as a warm little family group in a cosy, well-ordered home.

After a while, the Erhards started petitioning for the return of Bettina, and, when Bettina was four, the court sent her home.

One night, about a year later, an alarmed neighbor heard bloodcurdling screams from the Erhard house and called the police. Erhard was not at home when they arrived, but Mrs. Erhard was home, sprawled out dead-drunk on the sofa. The place was well-furnished and impeccably clean. A few objects had been overturned and broken. The children were found whimpering in their bedroom. Connie wasn't in bad shape, starved, slightly bruised, terrified. But Bettina's belly was swollen with malnutrition. Her body was a mass of contusions, lacerations, puncture wounds, sores, and old scars. There were rope marks around her ankles and wrists, and a gag mark across her mouth. One foot was so severely ulcerated that she could scarcely walk. Her hair was falling out, her skin deathly white, her eyes lifeless and dull.

In the course of the investigation and trial that followed, it was learned that the Erhards often bound and gagged Bettina before going off to their respective jobs. Little Connie had been spared that treatment, but she had not been spared the sight of her sister being tied up and whipped with steel wire or struck with sticks and high-heeled shoes. She had not been spared blows, or having to eat off the floor with her sister, when they were fed at all, or the terror that reigned in the household with the pleasant facade.

A jury sentenced Mrs. Erhard to three years in a women's reformatory. Charges against Lewis Erhard were, for some reason, dropped. One evening a moving van arrived. The contents of the nice little ranch house were removed and taken away, no one knows where. Erhard vanished simultaneously. The two little girls, Bettina, now five, and Connie, three, were placed with a foster family.

Mrs. Erhard served her time and was released, a contrite and chastened woman. She immediately started proceedings to regain custody of Connie. She wasn't interested in Bettina and didn't even want to see her. It was Connie she wanted.

In a series of hearings, Mrs. Erhard eloquently

pleaded her case and impressed the court with her sincerity. As a result, she was permitted visiting rights to the foster home in which her two children lived. At the judge's insistence, her visits were to be unsupervised so that she might have the best possible chance to establish a normal, relaxed relationship with her favorite child.

Bettina screamed, ran, and hid when she saw her mother coming, but that didn't matter. Mrs. Erhard didn't want to see her anyway. She wanted Connie. But little Connie, a bright six-year-old, was wary. She backed away, clutched her foster mother, and looked at her natural mother with dubious, frightened eyes.

But Mrs. Erhard persevered. Once a week, for more than three months, she came to visit Connie. After the first few visits, she would take the little girl out for several hours at a time, and bring her back. Connie seemed to have mixed feelings about these excursions with her natural mother. Before each visit she would be half-fascinated, half-afraid. Sometimes she came back happy, sometimes oddly silent. As time went by, Connie's foster mother began to sense a change in her. The child seemed nervous. Uneasily, the woman wondered what she should do about it.

She started wondering too late. One day Mrs. Erhard took Connie out for a longer trip than usual. Neither of them came back. They disappeared. Perhaps they joined Lewis Erhard. Nobody knows.

Bettina's scars have not yet healed. She limps. She bears the marks of many old wounds. She is withdrawn, timid, confused. Perhaps in time, with love, she will recover.[5]

[5] Vincent J. Fontana, M.D., *Somewhere a Child Is Crying* (Macmillan Publishing Co., 1973), pp. 2–3.

Can minors protect themselves against sexual abuse by parents or other adults?

When a parent takes sexual advantage of a child the crime is known as "incest." Sometimes a minor is sexually abused by other adult relatives or by a stepparent or guardian. The minor is in no way responsible for such a situation. The adult is at fault and the offense is a serious one. The minor should immediately report sexual abuse to a doctor, a clergyman or another reliable adult; or to *Child Abuse Careline*—a toll-free number listed in many telephone directories.

Can minors sue parents who injure them physically?

In legal terms, an injury or wrongful act committed by one person against another is called a "tort." A tort may be the basis for a lawsuit. If the local laws permit minors to sue their parents for a willful tort, the parents can be liable for assault and battery. But the courts are not in full agreement as to how these limits are defined. If minors believe they have been abused, they should call Child Abuse Careline (a toll-free number listed in telephone directories) immediately. A later step might be to consult a lawyer to find out about the possibility of taking court action.

What can happen to minors who leave home without their parents' consent?

American Jurisprudence Second makes the following statement:

The child until majority or emancipation has no right to leave the parental home and choose a different one though the law recognizes the natural diminution in parental control as the child reaches adolescence.[6]

This means simply that parents can insist that a minor stay home and if the minor does leave against the parents' wishes, the parent can have him or her returned with police aid.

From the financial standpoint, if a minor runs away from home because of abusive parents, the parents still have to support the child. On the other hand, if a minor leaves in order to be financially independent and to avoid parental authority, the parents usually are not obliged to provide support unless they previously agreed to do so. But there have been some cases where the parents were ordered by the court to support a minor even though he or she stayed away from home without their consent.

Do parents have control of the earnings of a minor?

This may come as a disappointment, but under the law parents have the right to the earnings of a minor child. This applies even if the minor does not live at home. Furthermore, as a minor, you cannot get around this by making a new employment contract or by assigning your wages to someone else. The reason underlying this parental right is that parents are obligated to support their children during their minority.

[6] *American Jurisprudence Second,* Vol. 59, Paragraph 74, p. 166.

Under some statutes, if your parents wish to obtain your earnings, they must notify your employer; if they do not, your wages legally belong to you.

A parent also has the right to assign your wages to someone else, which would mean that you would, in fact, receive nothing.

When a minor wins a lawsuit for injuries, to whom does the money belong?

The money belongs to the minor and this is true even in those cases where minors were required, because of their minority status, to have their parents or other adults bring the lawsuit for them.

If parents can afford it, are they obliged to send their children to college?

Until recently it was not necessary for parents to provide their children with a higher education. But this concept is changing. At present this is how the law regards it:

> . . . In determining what education is necessary for a particular child, consideration must be given to the progress of society and the attendant requirements on the citizen of today. And it has been pointed out that a college education was a rarity at the time of these early decisions [wherein the courts denied that this was a parent's obligation], but under modern conditions may be as necessary, especially for some callings, as an elementary or high school education formerly was. And the fact that the state maintains institutions of higher learning supported by public funds has been taken as indicating a public policy

that a college education should be available to all. Accordingly, the trend of recent authority is to the effect that under modern conditions and in proper cases, education beyond that provided in common schools may be a necessary which a parent is obliged to provide for his child, and that a parent able to do so may be required to bear the expense of a college education for a child evincing an aptitude therefore. Determination as to whether a parent should be so required in a particular case will depend on such factors as the financial condition of the parent, the statutory age of majority, whether the child is self-sustaining, and whether the parent has agreed to provide such education. A decree requiring a parent to pay for a college education for his child will not be entered where this will impose an undue hardship on the parent. A determination as to whether the parent should bear the expense of his child's education may be affected by the construction of statutory language in some instances.[7]

The following points should be noted: First, this opinion was based upon fairly recent court cases. Although there seems to be a strong trend toward making it obligatory for parents to finance their children's college expenses, there are many ifs, ands, and buts. Minors cannot definitely count on parents having to pay for higher education. For one thing, it is hard to judge when the expense would be an "undue hardship," unless parents are obviously rich.

Second, the judgement may depend upon whether

[7] *Ibid.*, Paragraph 59, p. 149.

or not the parents agreed previously to provide this education. If they didn't, the court may rule that they don't have to undertake the expense.

Third, some places have statutes which relieve parents of such an obligation under any circumstances.

Can parents force religious training on minors?

The answer is "Yes," with no exceptions. By law, religious training is solely under the parents' control and the courts have no authority to interfere. In fact, this right is so ensured that parents can make their wishes about it survive them to be carried out by a guardian. The only exceptions to this general rule come about when the parents' religious beliefs conflict with required medical treatment (operations, blood transfusions, etc.).

Do parents bear liability for criminal or civil acts committed by their minor children?

At common law, it is generally held that the mere fact of paternity does not make parents responsible for the torts (injuries or wrongs done to someone) of their minor children. The parents are not liable merely because the children live at home and are completely under their care.

But there are some circumstances where the parents may be held liable:

1. When the tort was committed by a minor at the direction of the parents.

2. Where the parents gave permission to commit the act.

3. Where the parents' own negligence made such a tort possible. For example, a parent may be liable if he or she lets a child handle a gun—or even leaves a gun where a child could get at it.

4. "The parent will incur liability for his minor child's intentional acts of violence or damage to persons or property if, knowing of the child's vicious or destructive tendencies or acts, he fails to exercise reasonable measures to restrain or discipline the child and thus encourages or acquiesces in such misconduct on the part of the child. . . ." [8]

[8] *Ibid.*, Paragraph 133, p. 234.

CHAPTER SEVEN

Drugs
and the Law

It may strike you as surprising that we have included alcohol in this chapter. But alcohol is a drug just as heroin, cocaine, opium, and opium derivatives are. However, for the sake of clarity, we are separating the laws about alcohol from those about marijuana, hashish, heroin, barbiturates, amphetamines, and the like, for this reason: many laws about alcohol, its purchase, and its use apply to minors alone, whereas those about the other drugs apply equally to minors and adults.

A few decades ago, from 1919 to 1933, alcohol was forbidden to every U.S. citizen. This was the era of the Eighteenth Amendment (Prohibition). But the law proved unenforceable; it was repealed and each state was allowed to have its own statutes regarding the sale and use of alcoholic beverages. Today local governments have their own individual laws, and there are a number of towns and counties which still do not permit bars or liquor stores.

Alcohol

Although age limitations vary from state to state, and in some instances vary according to the kind of beverage, every state in the union has laws about minors and liquor.

In general, the statutes consider it a crime to sell, furnish, give, or cause to be given or sold any intoxicating liquor to minors; and there are no constitutional grounds whereby a liquor dealer can successfully fight such a statute. The seller is not vindicated even if an adult pays for the liquor and then shares it with a companion who is known to be a minor.

In some states and under some statutes, the dealer is guilty even if he is ignorant of or mistaken about the age of the buyer. Hence you should understand why bartenders and liquor store dealers are so insistent on seeing proof of age. Now for specific replies to common questions.

What are the minimum age requirements for buying alcoholic beverages in the various states?

They are shown, by state, on page 98.

May adults buy drinks for minors in a bar or act as their agents in a liquor store?

A person who "treats" a minor by purchasing him a drink in a saloon has been declared to be equally guilty with the seller . . . and conversely, a saloonkeeper who sells to an adult treating a minor in his company is guilty of dealing or trafficking in intoxicants with a minor.[1]

This applies also to an adult making a purchase

---

[1] *American Jurisprudence Second*, Vol. 45, Paragraph 268, p. 671.

Minimum Legal Age for Purchase of Alcoholic Beverages

In the United States and Canada

	Years		Years
Alabama	21	New Brunswick	21
Alaska	19	Newfoundland	21
Alberta	18	New Hampshire	18
Arizona	19	New Jersey	18
Arkansas	21	New Mexico	21
British Columbia	19	New York	18
California	21	North Carolina (b)	21
Colorado (c)	21	North Dakota	21
Connecticut	18	Northwest Territories	19
Delaware	20	Nova Scotia	19
Dist. of Col. (b)	21	Ohio (c)	21
Florida	18	Oklahoma (d)	21
Georgia	18	Ontario	18
Hawaii	18	Oregon	21
Idaho	19	Pennsylvania	21
Illinois	21	Prince Edward Island	18
Indiana	21	Quebec	18
Iowa	18	Rhode Island	18
Kansas (c)	21	Saskatchewan	19
Kentucky	21	South Carolina (e)	21
Louisiana	18	South Dakota (g)	21
Maine	18	Tennessee	18
Manitoba	18	Texas	18
Maryland	21	Utah	21
Massachusetts	18	Vermont	18
Michigan	18	Virginia (c)	21
Minnesota	21	Washington	21
Mississippi (h)	21	West Virginia	18
Missouri	21	Wisconsin	18
Montana	18	Wyoming	19
Nebraska	19	Yukon Territory	19
Nevada	21		

(b) Light wine, beer 18. (c) 3.2 beer 18. (d) 3.2 beer: male 21; female 18. (e) Beer and wine 18. (g) 3.2 beer. (h) Beer not over 4 percent by weight 18.

for a minor in a liquor store with or without the knowledge of the vendor. And both parties are guilty.

May minors purchase liquor for adults?

Usually, no. Because the statutes prohibiting the

sale of liquor to minors are so strictly worded and so severely enforced, it is usually no excuse that the minor was in fact purchasing the liquor for an adult.

There are statutes in some places which permit such a purchase if the minor has the written consent of a parent or guardian. But the chances are slim that a liquor store will sell you liquor even with written consent. It is too risky.

May minors buy alcoholic drinks for themselves at a bar if they have the written consent of parents or guardians?

Yes, in some states—but written consent is required each time.

> Some states prohibiting the sale or gift of intoxicating liquor to minors make an exception where such sale or gift is made with the written consent of their parents or guardians.
>
> . . . . It has been held that the parental consent must be for each occasion, and that a general permit to drink or obtain liquor in a specified barroom without limitation as to time or quantity is void, since it violates the underlying theory of such legislation that the state, and not the parent alone, is concerned in the protection of minors from the liquor evil, and since to permit such a general consent would be to suffer a frustration of the purpose of the statute.[2]

May minors purchase liquor out of state where their age makes such a purchase permissible?

[2] *Ibid.*, Paragraph 270, p. 673.

Generally, they may. The law of their state of residence does not apply to the state where they purchase the liquor. But if minors order liquor out of state by mail, and the dealer delivers the liquor to the minors' home, the dealer is guilty under the law of the state where he made the delivery. This same regulation would apply to a phone order.

May parents or other adults serve drinks to minors in their (the adults') home?

If there are statutes in the state forbidding the sale or gift of liquor to minors, the adults are technically committing a crime. This law is sometimes enforced by zealous police officers. Such was the case in Darien, Conn., a few years ago. The parents were arrested for serving liquor to minors at a party in their house. However, the law is not always interpreted so strictly:

> . . . . Statutes forbidding the giving or selling of intoxicating liquor to minors have been held to refer only to commercial transactions or transactions connected in some way with commerce in liquor and to have no application to the situation where a minor is given alcohol in a private home as an act of personal hospitality.[3]

In fact the law is rather vague on this point. Here is a fairly typical court case:

The defendant, Dorothy M., was convicted in a

[3] *Ibid.*

lower court of serving alcoholic beverages to four minor girls over a period of six months. She appealed the conviction. The Appeals Court judge, in reversing the conviction, stated: ". . . There was proof that at various times over a period of six months she permitted four children under the ages of eighteen to congregate in her home and there gave them alcoholic beverages to drink. Her defense on the law, however, is that it was not the legislative intent to make criminal the service of alcoholic beverages to youngsters in the home of the person who served them. The point is well taken and the conviction must be reversed and the indictment dismissed."

So you see, the law varies from place to place, as to content, interpretation, and enforcement.

Other Drugs

Almost simultaneously with the repeal of Prohibition—as if the law felt itself deprived of the opportunity for moral meddling—the Uniform Narcotic Drug Act of 1932 was passed. It was initiated by the Federal Bureau of Narcotics, whose chief succeeded in persuading the lawmakers that marijuana was a vicious drug responsible for acts of sexual perversion and crimes of violence.

Despite the fact that this was later refuted by medical science, the federal and state laws about marijuana remained disproportionately harsh for years. To add to the injustice, penalties varied absurdly from state to state. For example, back in 1973, in Illinois the use of marijuana was a misdemeanor entailing ninety days to one year in jail. In Nebraska possession of less than eight ounces brought only a seven-day jail sentence with instruction in drug abuse. In Texas, the possession of marijuana brought imprisonment for two years to life—and a second offense brought ten years to life with no suspension, probation or parole. In Virginia, the penalty for possessing marijuana was imprisonment for not less than three nor more than five years.

Fortunately, in the past few years such discrepancies have been recognized as unfair. In addition, there has been a growing recognition that marijuana is comparatively harmless compared to hard drugs such as heroin. Furthermore, the courts have seen the need for change and for some semblance of national uniformity in drug laws. Thus in 1970 the Drug Abuse and Control Act was drafted. Each state was free to adopt it or not. It is not a federal law. A law journal describes its purposes as follows:

> This Uniform Act was drafted to achieve uniformity between the laws of the several States and those of the Federal government. It has been designed to complement the new Federal narcotic and dangerous drug legislation and provide an interlocking trellis of Federal and State law to enable government at all levels to control more effectively the drug abuse problem.

> The exploding drug abuse problem in the past

ten years has reached epidemic proportions. No longer is the problem confined to a few major cities or to a particular economic group. Today it encompasses almost every nationality, race, and economic level. It has moved from the major urban areas into the suburban and even rural communities, and has manifested itself in every State in the Union.

Much of this major increase in drug use and abuse is attributable to the increased mobility of our citizens and their affluence. As modern American society becomes increasingly mobile, drugs clandestinely manufactured or illegally diverted from legitimate channels in one part of a State are easily transported for sale to another part of that State or even to another State. Nowhere is this mobility manifested with greater impact than in the legitimate pharmaceutical industry. The lines of distribution of the products of this major national industry cross in and out of a State innumerable times during the manufacturing or distribution processes. To assure the continued free movement of controlled substances between States, while at the same time securing such States against drug diversion from legitimate sources, it becomes critical to approach not only the control of illicit and legitimate traffic in these substances at the national and international levels, but also to approach this problem at the State and local level on a uniform basis.

A main objective of this Uniform Act is to create a coordinated and codified system of drug control, similar to that utilized at the Federal level, which classifies all narcotics, marihuana, and dangerous drugs subject to control into five schedules, with each schedule having its own criteria for drug placement. This classification system will enable the agency charged with implementing it to add, delete, or reschedule substances based upon new scientific findings and the abuse potential of the substance.

Another objective of this Act is to establish a closed regulatory system for the legitimate handlers of controlled drugs in order better to prevent illicit drug diversion. This system will require that these individuals register with a designated State agency, maintain records, and make biennial inventories of all controlled drug stocks.

The Act sets out the prohibited activities in detail, but does not prescribe specific fines or sentences, this being left to the discretion of the individual States. It further provides innovative law enforcement tools to improve investigative efforts and provides for interim education and training programs relating to the drug abuse problem.

The Uniform Act updates and improves existing State laws and insures legislative and administrative flexibility to enable the States to cope with both present and future drug problems. It is recognized that law enforcement may not be the ultimate solution to the drug abuse program. It is hoped that present research efforts will be continued and vigorously expanded, particularly as they relate to the development of rehabilitation, treatment, and educational programs for addicts, drug dependent persons, and potential drug abusers.[4]

The following states have now adopted the Uniform Controlled Substances Act:

[4] *Uniform Laws Annotated* (West Publishing Co., 1973), pp. 146–147.

Alabama	Nevada
Arkansas	New Jersey
California	New Mexico
Connecticut	New York
Delaware	North Carolina
Florida	North Dakota
Georgia	Ohio
Hawaii	Oklahoma
Idaho	Pennsylvania
Illinois	Puerto Rico
Indiana	Rhode Island
Iowa	South Carolina
Kansas	South Dakota
Kentucky	Tennessee
Louisiana	Texas
Maryland	Utah
Massachusetts	Virgin Islands
Michigan	Virginia
Minnesota	Washington
Mississippi	West Virginia
Missouri	Wisconsin
Montana	Wyoming
Nebraska	

In simple, everyday language, what does its adoption by forty-four states mean? Not as much uniformity as one might hope, but some real improvements:

1. It has started a trend to bring about the decriminalization of marijuana laws. Thus in most states possession of small amounts (less than one ounce of marijuana) is now classified as a misdemeanor.

2. It has initiated a trend toward greater leniency for first offenders. If a person has not been previously convicted under any law relating to marijuana, but is found guilty of possessing a small amount, the court may defer any further proceedings and place the person on probation for a period of time. If the accused

reports regularly to the probation officer and has not committed any further offense by the end of the probation period, the court may discharge him, or her, and dismiss proceedings. In this case, the offense will not be recorded as a conviction, and the person's record will remain clear. (Such leniency, however, applies only once.)

3. When an offender has more than a small amount of marijuana (usually more than an ounce) on his person and is apprehended in a public place, the law generally assumes that such possession is for the purpose of sale or distribution. In such a case the penalty is more severe. Most states make distinctions according to the amount of marijuana possessed— greater amounts drawing more severe penalties.

The laws are not uniform yet, however—even among states that have adopted the Uniform Controlled Substances Act. For example, a number of states have not followed the UCSA's pattern of doubling the penalty for second offenders. As a result, penalties for second offenses vary a good deal among the states.

Here are some legal terms which you should understand as they apply to drug laws.

FELONY: This is the word for a serious crime which merits a severe punishment.
MISDEMEANOR: A misdemeanor carries a less severe punishment than a felony. The distinction between *felony* and *misdemeanor* often varies in different states. One state may have a law which says that

possession of marijuana is punishable by a week in the county jail. Another state may give two years in a state prison. In the first case, possession is a misdemeanor; in the second, it is a felony.

POSSESSION: This means having control over something, or seeming to. For example (and this could apply to liquor as well), if a law officer finds marijuana in your car or on your person, it is assumed that you are the possessor—that is, you exercise control over it—and it is up to you to prove otherwise.

USE: There are some states which have different penalties for use and for possession. Use sometimes results in a lesser sentence.

FURNISHING: This means the transfer of drugs from one person to another such as "passing a joint." It does not mean *sale* of drugs.

SUSPENSION: When accused persons, after having been found guilty, get a "suspended sentence," the sentence does not have to be served immediately. Instead, they are put on probation, a trial period which is usually longer than the sentence itself. However, if they break the law, even during the last week of the suspended sentence, they must serve the whole sentence in addition to a new one. Many states do not allow suspended sentences for drug offenses —including offenses involving marijuana.

PROBATION: This means that a person, convicted of a crime, has freedom depending on good behavior. Probation may be granted along with a suspended sentence or by itself. When granted by itself it is called straight probation. To illustrate: if you were convicted of possession of marijuana and were given a two-year straight probation, you would have to obey the specific terms of your probation as established by the probation officer or by the court. You would keep the probation officer informed of where you go and what you do. Other conditions might include having to be home by a certain time, consulting a psychiatrist, attending a drug clinic, or even going to school.

The following list of statutes, state-by-state, is very simplified and is confined to possession, not to sale or distribution of marijuana. Since state statutes are continually changing, we have listed, for each state, the Title number and Section number in the state's statute book. You can take this information to your local library and check for yourself on current changes, if any. Practically every library is supplied with the most recent state statute book. Those states in the following list which are prefixed with "C.D." are those which may allow a first offender a conditional discharge. The decision is up to the judge or presiding official.

Laws About Marijuana Possession, State by State

Alabama–Code of Ala. Tit. 22, Sec. 258
>Law modeled on Uniform Controlled Substances Act.
>Possession, any amt., 0–1 yr., and/or $1,000 fine.

(C.D.) Alaska–Laws, Chap. 110 Sec. 1 (1975)
>Possession, any amt. in private for personal use, or up to 1 oz. in public, $100 fine only.
>Possession, more than 1 oz. in public, 0–1 yr. and/or $1,000 fine.

Arizona–Rev. Stat. Ann. Sec. 36-1002 (1974)
　　Possession, any amt., 0–1 yr. and/or $1,000 fine.

(C.D.) Arkansas–Stat. Sec. 82-1001 and 82-2601 (1976)
　　Law modeled on Uniform Controlled Substances Act.
　　Possession, any amt., 0–1 yr. and/or $250 fine.

(C.D.) California–West's Ann. Health & Safety Code, Sec.
　11000 to 11651
　　Law modeled on Uniform Controlled Substances Act.
　　Possession, up to 1 oz., $100 fine only.
　　Possession over 1 oz., 0–6 mos. and/or $500 fine.

(C.D.) Colorado–Colorado Acts, Chap. 115, Sec. 7 (1975)
　(Narcotic Drug Act)
　　Possession, up to 1 oz., $100 fine only.
　　Possession over 1 oz., 0–1 yr. and/or $500 fine.

(C.D.) Connecticut–Gen. Stat. Ann., Sec. 19-443 to 19-504
　　Law modeled on Uniform Controlled Substances Act.
　　Possession, up to 4 oz., 0–1 yr. and/or $1,000 fine.
　　Possession over 4 oz., 0–5 yrs. and/or $2,000 fine.

(C.D.) Delaware–16 Del. Code, Sec. 4701-4778
　　Law modeled on Uniform Controlled Substances Act.
　　Possession, any amt., 0–2 yrs. and/or $500 fine.

(C.D.) D.C.–Title 33-401-417 (Narcotic Drug Act)
　　Possession, 0–1 yr. and/or $100–$1,000 fine.

(C.D.) Florida–Stat. Ann. Sec. 893.01 to 893.15
　　Law modeled on Uniform Controlled Substances Act.
　　Possession, under 5 grams, 0–1 yr. and/or $1,000 fine.
　　Possession, over 5 grams, 0–2 yrs. and/or $1,000 fine.

(C.D.) Georgia–Code Ann. Secs. 79A-801 to 79A-834, 79A-9917

Law modeled on Uniform Controlled Substances Act.
Possession, up to 1 oz., 0–1 yr. and/or $1,000 fine.
Possession, over 1 oz., 1–10 yrs.

Hawaii–H.R.S. Secs. 329-1 to 329-58 (1975)

Law modeled on Uniform Controlled Substances Act.
Possession, up to 1 oz., 0–30 days and/or $500 fine.
Possession, over 1 oz., 0–1 yr. and/or $1,000 fine.

(C.D.) Idaho–Code 37-2701–37-2751

Law modeled on Uniform Controlled Substances Act.
Possession, up to 3 oz., 0–1 yr and/or $1,000 fine.
Possession, over 3 oz., 0–5 yrs. and/or $15,000 fine.

(C.D.) Illinois–Ann. Stat. Ch. 56½, Sec. 1100 to 1603 (Smith Hurd Supp. 1975)

Law modeled on Uniform Controlled Substances Act.
Possession, 10–30 grams, 0–1 yr. and/or $1,000 fine.
Possession, 30–500 grams, 1–3 yrs. and/or $10,000 fine.

(C.D.) Indiana–Ann. Stat. Sec. 10-3561 (Supp. 1975)

Law modeled on Uniform Controlled Substances Act.
Possession, up to 30 grams, 0–1 yr. and/or $5,000 fine.
Possession, over 30 grams, 2–4 yrs. and/or $10,000 fine.

(C.D.) Iowa–Code Ann. Sec. 204.101 to 204.502, 409 (1) (Supp. 1975-76)

Law modeled on Uniform Controlled Substances Act.
Possession, any amount, 0–6 mos. and/or $1,000 fine.

Kansas–Stat. Ann., Sec. 65-4172a, b, 21-4501 (Supp. 1974)
Law modeled on Uniform Controlled Substances Act.
Possession, any amount, 0–1 yr. and/or $2,500 fine.

(C.D.) Kentucky–Rev. Stat. Ann. Sec. 218A 990 (6) (k), 7 (h)
(Supp. 1974)
Law modeled on Uniform Controlled Substances Act.
Possession, any amt., 0–90 days and/or $250 fine.

(C.D.) Louisiana–Rev. Stat. Sec. 40.983 (Supp. 1976)
Law modeled on Uniform Controlled Substances Act.
Possession, any amt., 0–1 yr. and/or $500 fine.

(C.D.) Maine–Rev. Stat. Ann. Title 22, Sec. 2383 (Supp.
1975) (Narcotic Drug Act)
Possession, any amt. for personal use, $200 fine only.

(C.D.) Maryland–Ann. Code, Art. 27, Sec. 292 (a)-(b) (Supp.
1975)
Law modeled on Uniform Controlled Substances Act.
Possession, any amt., 0–1 yr. and/or $1,000 fine.

(C.D.) Massachusetts–Gen. Laws Ann. Ch. 94C, Sec. 34
(1975)
Law modeled on Uniform Controlled Substances Act.
Possession, any amt., 0–6 mos. and/or $500 fine.

(C.D.) Michigan–Compiled Laws Ann. Sec. 335-347 (1)
(1975)
Law modeled on Uniform Controlled Substances Act.
Possession, up to 2 oz., 0–1 yr. and/or $1,000 fine.
Possession, over 2 oz., 0–4 yrs. and/or $2,000 fine.

(C.D.) Minnesota–Stat. Ann. Sec. 152.18 (1) (2) (Supp. 1976)

> Law modeled on Uniform Controlled Substances Act.
> Possession, up to 1½ oz., $100 fine only.
> Possession, over 1½ oz., 0–3 yrs. and/or $3,000 fine.

(C.D.) Mississippi–Code Ann. Secs. 41029-150 (c) (1) (2) (Supp. 1973)

> Law modeled on Uniform Controlled Substances Act.
> Possession, up to 1 oz., $250 fine only.
> Possession, over 1 oz., 0–1 yr. and/or $1,000 fine.

(C.D.) Missouri–Ann. Stat. Sec. 195-200 (1) (a) (b) (2) (4) (5) (Vernon Supp. 1976)

> Law modeled on Uniform Controlled Substances Act.
> Possession, up to 35 grams, 0–1 yr. and/or $1,000 fine.
> Possession, over 35 grams, 0–5 yrs. and/or $1,000 fine.

Montana–Rev. Code Ann. Sec. 54-132 (b) 133 (a)-(c) (Supp. 1974)

> Law modeled on Uniform Controlled Substances Act.
> Possession, up to 60 grams, 0–1 yr. and/or $1,000 fine.
> Possession, over 60 grams, 0–5 yrs. and/or $1,000 fine.

Nebraska–Rev. Stat. Sec. 28-4, 125 (1) (5) (Cum. Supp. 1975)

> Law modeled on Uniform Controlled Substances Act.
> Possession, up to 1 lb., 0–7 days and/or $500 fine.
> Possession, over 1 lb., 0–1 yr. and/or $500 fine.

(C.D.) Nevada–Rev. Stat., Sec. 453.321 (2) .336. (1) (2) (a)-(b) (1973)

Law modeled on Uniform Controlled Substances Act.
Possession, any amt. by person over 21, 1–6 yrs. and/or $2,000 fine.
Possession, up to 1 oz. by person under 21, 0–1 yr. and/or $1,000 fine.

New Hampshire–Rev. Stat. Ann. Sec. 318, B-26(I) (a)-(c) Supp. 1975 Sec. 651.2 (1974)
Possession up to 1 lb., 0–1 yr. and/or $500 fine.
Possession over 1 lb., 0–7 yrs. and/or $2,000 fine.

New Jersey–Stat. Ann. Sec. 2A: 169-4 (1971) Sec. 24:21 et seq. (Supp. 1975)
Law modeled on Uniform Controlled Substances Act.
Possession, up to 25 grams, 0–6 mos. and/or $500 fine.
Possession, over 25 grams, 0–5 yrs. and/or $15,000 fine.

(C.D.) New Mexico–Stat. Ann. Secs. 40A-29-3 (A) (D) (1972) Secs. 54-11-20, 23 (Supp. 1973)
Law modeled on Uniform Controlled Substances Act.
Possession, up to 1 oz., 0–15 days and/or $50–$100 fine.
Possession, 1 to 8 oz., 0–1 yr. and/or $100–$1,000 fine.

New York–Penal Law, Sec. 220.00-60 (McKinney Supp. 1974-75) see also Sec. 70.00 (McKinney 1975)
Law modeled on Uniform Controlled Substances Act.
Possession, up to 25 grams, $100 fine only.
Possession, over 25 grams, 0–3 mos. or $500 fine.

(C.D.) North Carolina–Gen. Stat. Sec. 90-96 (a) (b) (1975)
Law modeled on Uniform Controlled Substances Act.

Possession, up to 1 oz., 0–6 mos. and/or $500 fine.
Possession, over 1 oz., 0–5 yrs. and/or $5,000 fine.

(C.D.) North Dakota–Cent. Code Sec. 19-03.1-30 (Supp. 1975)
Law modeled on Uniform Controlled Substances Act.
Possession, any amt., 0–1 yr. and/or $1,000 fine.

(C.D.) Ohio–Baldwin's Ohio Rev. Code, Sec. 3719.01 to 3719.99
Law modeled on Uniform Controlled Substances Act.
Possession, up to 100 grams, $100 fine only.
Possession, 100 to 200 grams, 0–30 days and/or $250 fine.
Possession, 200 to 600 grams, 6 mos.–5 yrs. and/or $2,500 fine.

(C.D.) Oklahoma–Stat. Ann. Title 63, Sec. 2-401 (1973)
Law modeled on Uniform Controlled Substances Act.
Possession, any amt., 0–1 yr.

(C.D.) Oregon–Rev. Stat. Sec. 167-207 (1974) (Narcotic Drug Act)
Possession, up to 1 oz., $100 fine only.
Possession, over 1 oz., 0–10 yrs. and/or $2,500 fine.

(C.D.) Pennsylvania–Stat. Ann. Title 35, Sec. 780-117 (Supp. 1975-76)
Law modeled on Uniform Controlled Substances Act.
Possession, up to 30 grams, 0–30 days and/or $500 fine.
Possession, over 30 grams, 0–1 yr. and/or $5,000 fine.

Puerto Rico–Vol. 24, Laws of Puerto Rico, Ann. Secs. 2101–2607.
> Law modeled on Uniform Controlled Substances Act.
> Possession, 0–5 years and/or $5,000 fine.

Rhode Island–Gen. Law Ann. Sec. 21-28-4.01 (A) (B) (C) 2102804.11 (Cum Supp. 1975)
> Law modeled on Uniform Controlled Substances Act.
> Possession, any amt., 0–1 yr. and/or $500 fine.

(C.D.) South Carolina–Code Ann. Sec. 32-1510.57 (a)-(b) (Supp. 1975)
> Law modeled on Uniform Controlled Substances Act.
> Possession, up to 1 oz., 0–3 mos. and/or $100 fine.
> Possession, over 1 oz., 0–6 mos. and/or $1,000 fine.

South Dakota–Compiled Laws Ann. Sec. 39-17-113 & 114 (Supp. 1975)
> Law modeled on Uniform Controlled Substances Act.
> Possession, up to 1 oz., 0–30 days and/or $100 fine.
> Possession, over 1 oz., 0–1 yr. and/or $1,000 fine.

(C.D.) Tennessee–Code Ann. Sec. 52-1432-1434 (Supp. 1975)
> Law modeled on Uniform Controlled Substances Act.
> Possession, any amt., 0–1 yr. and/or $1,000 fine.

(C.D.) Texas–Rev. Civil Stat., Art. 4476-15, sec. 4.12 (Supp. 1975-76)
> Law modeled on Uniform Controlled Substances Act.
> Possession, up to 2 oz., 0–6 mos. and/or $1,000 fine.
> Possession, 2–4 oz., 0–1 yr. and/or $2,000 fine.

(C.D.) Utah–Code Ann. Sec. 58-37-8 (10) (1974)

Law modeled on Uniform Controlled Substances Act.
Possession, any amt., 0–6 mos. and/or $299 fine.

Vermont–Stat. Ann. Title 18, Sec. 4224 (Supp. 1975)
Possession, any amt., 0–6 mos. and/or $500 fine.

Virgin Islands–Vol. 19, Virgin Island Code. Sec. 591.
Law modeled on Uniform Controlled Substances Act.
Possession, 0–1 year and/or $5,000 fine.

(C.D.) Virginia–Code Ann. Sec. 18.2-251 (1975)
Law modeled on Uniform Controlled Substances Act.
Possession, any amt., 0–1 yr. and/or $1,000 fine.

Washington–Rev. Code Ann. Sec. 69.50, 401 (a) (1) et seq.
Law modeled on Uniform Controlled Substances Act.
Possession, up to 40 grams, 0–90 days and/or $250
fine.
Possession, over 40 grams, 0–5 yrs. and/or $10,000
fine.

(C.D.) West Virginia–Code Ann. Sec. 60-A-4-407 (Supp.
1975)
Law modeled on Uniform Controlled Substances Act.
Possession, any amt., 90 days–6 mos. and/or $1,000
fine.

(C.D.) Wisconsin–Stat. Ann. Sec. 161.47 (1) (1974)
Law modeled on Uniform Controlled Substances Act.
Possession, any amt., 0–1 yr. and/or $250 fine.

(C.D.) Wyoming–Stat. Ann. Sec. 35-347.37 (Supp. 1975)
Law modeled on Uniform Controlled Substances Act.
Possession, any amt., 0–6 mos. and/or $1,000 fine.

CHAPTER EIGHT

If You Are Arrested— Criminal Law and the Minor

Up to this point, you have learned what the penalties may be for committing certain crimes in terms of fines and prison sentences. In most cases the penalties are the same for minors and adults. It is now very important to learn how to handle yourself—as a minor —if you are arrested. What are your rights? What, if any, difference exists between being accused as a criminal or as a juvenile delinquent?

In the last decade of the nineteenth century, European and American children were tried in the same courts, and sentenced to the same prisons, as adults. For example, in Great Britain, just before the turn of the twentieth century, a seven-year-old could be convicted of a crime. This was also the case in some of our American states. Even at the beginning of the twentieth century, children were executed for crimes; for example, an eight-year-old was executed for arson, and a thirteen-year-old for murder.

In Massachusetts in 1877, a movement to separate child offenders from adult offenders was started. And in Illinois in 1899, a most significant contribution was made by establishing a juvenile court system which applied to children over twelve and under sixteen. Until that time, children in Illinois were tried and jailed like adult offenders. Just before this new system in Chicago in 1899, 332 boys from nine to sixteen were sent to the city prison. They were committed under the blanket charge of "disorderly conduct," which covered almost everything from burglary and assault with a deadly weapon, to picking up coal on the railroad tracks, "flipping trains" (hopping on and off moving cars), and setting bonfires or playing ball in the street. These children were sent to Bridewell —a jail notorious for its horrible conditions. Indeed, even in those days, police judges sometimes pardoned child offenders rather than send them there.

The establishment of a juvenile court system in Illinois and later in other states helped to ease the condition of juvenile offenders. However, the benefits of separate juvenile courts for youthful offenders have failed in many areas. This often happens when the courts try to patch up an injustice rather than get at a basic social reform.

In a speech in 1968, Supreme Court Justice William O. Douglas summed up some of the problems:

The juvenile court was to be a clinic, not a court: the judge and all of the attendants were to be visualized as white-coated experts there to supervise, enlighten, and cure—not to punish.

This new agency—which stood in the shoes of the parent or guardian—was to draw on all the medical, psychological, and psychiatric knowledge of the day and transform the delinquent. These experts, motivated by love, were to transform troubled children into normal ones, saving them from criminal careers.

I'm not sure as to all that went wrong. But I do know several things. First, municipal budgets were not equal to the task of enticing experts to work in this field in large numbers. Second, such experts as we had, notably the psychiatrists and analysts, were drawn to the flesh pots, receiving handsome fees for rehabilitating the rich. Third, the love and tenderness possessed by the white-coated judge and attendants were not sufficient to untangle the web of subconscious influences that possessed the troubled youngsters. Fourth, correctional institutions that were designed to care for these delinquents often became miniature prisons with many of the same vicious aspects. Fifth, the secrecy of the juvenile proceedings led to much overreaching and arbitrary actions. Absolute power is a heady thing even when bestowed on men of good intention.[1]

In 1968 a survey (made by Dr. Samuel A. Kramer) of 1,214 juvenile courts across the country disclosed that over 31,000 children picked up by the police were held in adult jails to await action. In addition, 20,000 were kept in juvenile detention homes. If they had been adults, they would probably have been out on bail. This situation has not improved.

Nevertheless, three important decisions led the way to defining a minor's basic rights in juvenile court. These were U.S. Supreme Court decisions: *Kent* v. *United States (1966); In re Gault (1969); and In the Matter of Samuel Winship (1969).*

[1] *Juvenile Court Judges Journal,* 19(1), Spring 1968.

The Kent decision dealt with a very specific issue: when and how a court may transfer a juvenile suspected of a serious offense to a general criminal court for trial.

The court [the U.S. Supreme Court] was emphatic that the waiver of jurisdiction [that is, the minor's giving up his right to be tried in juvenile court] was a "critically important" action to the juvenile because there are special rights and immunities that accrue from juvenile court handling. The juvenile is shielded from publicity; he or she may be confined, but, with rare exceptions, may not be jailed along with adults. He or she may be detained, but only until the age of twenty-one. The child is protected against consequences of adult conviction—such consequences as the loss of civil rights, the use of a court record against him in subsequent proceedings, and disqualification for public employment.[2]

Therefore, to make as certain as possible that a juvenile offender voluntarily and knowingly agreed to have his trial transferred from a juvenile court, the U.S. Supreme Court set forth these conditions which would permit a waiver by the minor:

(1) A hearing must be held on a motion for a waiver . . . [which] must measure up to the essentials of due process and fair treatment; (2) a full investigation must be made and should include pertinent back-

[2] *Juvenile Justice,* National Council of Juvenile Court Judges, May 1973, Vol. 24, No. 1, p. 3.

ground information on the juvenile; i.e., social stud-
ies, evaluations and probation reports, or similar
records for consideration by the court; (3) the child
is entitled to be represented by counsel, and his attorney shall have full access to all of the records and
reports considered or relied upon by the court, and
also have the opportunity to cross-examine and re-
fute any of the reports; (4) the court must "accom-
pany its waiver order with a statement of the reasons
of consideration therefore sufficient to demonstrate
that a full investigation had been made, and must set
forth the basis for the order with sufficient specificity
to permit meaningful review." [3]

The *Gault* decision involved a fifteen-year-old
(Gerald Gault) who was accused and convicted of
using obscene language over the phone to a woman.
He was tried under the juvenile court system of the
time and sentenced to remain in an industrial school
for six years (until the age of twenty-one). His case
was appealed all the way up to the U.S. Supreme
Court where he won the appeal.

The Supreme Court ruled . . . in effect that (1) he
[a juvenile] is entitled to fair notice of the charges
against him, (2) he has a right to representation by
legal counsel, and (3) he is entitled to cross examination of witnesses, and further to be free from self-
incrimination. [4]

[3] *Ibid.*, p. 4.
[4] *Ibid.*

Gault had not been given any of these rights. However, even this decision did not clearly establish that a juvenile was entitled to all the procedural guarantees allowed an adult charged with a crime.

The *Winship* decision in 1969 went a step further. This case established the principle that the prosecution must follow the same rules regarding proof "beyond a reasonable doubt" in juvenile court that have always been applied in adult proceedings.

There is growing recognition that the juvenile court system is often unfair, and some states are trying to change the system. A typical example is Connecticut's Youthful Offenders Act of 1971. Here are some of the provisions of this act.

Section 1. For the purpose of this act, "youth" means a minor who has reached the age of sixteen years but has not reached the age of eighteen; and "youthful offender" means a youth who has committed a crime or crimes which are not class A felonies (murder or kidnapping) who has not previously been convicted of a felony, or been previously adjudged a youthful offender. . . .

Notice that age is spelled out. (Each state has its own age limits for defining a minor.) Notice also, that the term "juvenile delinquent," which had become synonymous with "criminal," is not used.

Section 2. . . . An investigation be made of such defendant for the purpose of determining whether he is eligible to be adjudged a youthful offender.

In other words, not everyone between the ages of sixteen and eighteen has this privilege. If one has a previous record, the trial will be held in an adult court.

> Section 5. No statement, admission or confession made by the defendant to the court or to any person designated by the court to conduct the examination, investigation and questioning . . . shall ever be admissible as evidence against him or his interest, except that the court may take such statement, admission or confession into consideration at the time of sentencing such defendant, if defendant has been adjudged a youthful offender, or has been found guilty of the crime charged. . . .

This means you can't testify against yourself. (But, if you're convicted, the judge can then take note of any admissions you made, and his sentence may be affected by them.)

> Section 7. . . . If such defendant is committed while such examination and investigation is pending, before trial, during trial or after judgement and before sentence, those persons in charge of the place of detention shall segregate such defendant, to the extent of their facilities, from defendants over the age of eighteen years charged with crimes.

In other words, Section 7 intended that a juvenile defendant be separated from adults who were charged with crimes. But remember the phrase, "to the extent of their facilities." This means that juveniles can be jailed with adults when no other facilities are available. And since funds for improving prisons are limited, juveniles often do end up in cells with adult criminals.

> Section 10. No determination made under the provisions of this act shall operate as a disqualification of any youth subsequently to hold public office or public employment, or, as a forfeiture of any right or privilege to receive any license granted by public authority and no youth shall be denominated a criminal by reason of such determination, nor shall such determination be deemed a conviction.

This is probably the most protective provision of this act. Notice that the word "determination" rather than "conviction" is used. It means that a youthful offender does not have a record as a criminal. So a juvenile loses no rights of citizenship, and, theoretically at least, has a clean slate.

As a result of continuing changes and innovations in juvenile court procedures the line of demarcation and the difference between these procedures and criminal court procedures is becoming less and less distinguishable. In addition, the age at which minors are afforded the immunities of the juvenile courts varies from state to state and there are numerous instances wherein a minor may be transferred for trial to a criminal court. Therefore the following questions and answers refer chiefly to adult criminal court procedure.

When can you be arrested?

A policeman may arrest you without a warrant under the following circumstances:

1. If he sees you commit or try to commit a violation of the law.

2. If a felony or certain misdemeanor has been committed, and the policeman has reasonable grounds to believe you did it (even if he was not there at the time).

When must a policeman have a warrant to make an arrest?

In general, a policeman must have a warrant to arrest you for a misdemeanor if he himself does not see you do it. But he does not need a warrant to arrest you for a felony if he has reasonable grounds to believe you committed it.

What is a warrant?

A warrant is an order signed by a magistrate or judge. It is made after the judge has heard a complaint by someone, usually the police, which charges that you committed a crime. The judge will issue the warrant only if there is good reason to believe you committed the crime. It must state the charge against you and it tells the policeman to arrest you and bring you before a magistrate or judge. In the case of a misdemeanor (as contrasted to a felony), you cannot be arrested on a warrant on Sunday, or at night, unless the magistrate or judge says so in the warrant itself. If a policeman has a warrant for your arrest, he must tell you he has it. You have the right to see it and he must show it to you.

Can a policeman use force to arrest you?

A policeman may use enough force to arrest you if you resist. But, after you have been restrained, he may not continue to use force.

In order to make a lawful arrest or to serve a warrant, a policeman may break open a door or window if you refuse to let him in.

What happens after you are arrested?

You are taken to a police station. There a record of your arrest and the charge against you must be reported without unnecessary delay. Before questioning you, the police must tell you what the charge is. In some states, you will be fingerprinted and photographed.

Do you have to answer questions?

These are your rights (and the police must tell you what your rights are):

1. You have the right not to make any statements about the offense charged against you.

2. If you do make any statements they can and will be used against you.

3. You have the right to have a lawyer represent you, and also the right to have time to discuss your case with him or her.

4. If you decide to answer questions without your lawyer present, you still have the right to stop answering at any time.

5. You also have the right to stop answering at any time until you talk to your lawyer.

6. If you do not have the money to hire a lawyer, a lawyer may be appointed by the court to represent you.

What can you do if force is used to make you answer questions?

You should report this immediately to your lawyer and to the district attorney. Any injuries and bruises suffered by you should also be reported promptly to the court.

Does a policeman's offer to help you, or intervene with the court in exchange for a confession by you, mean anything?

No, it does not. His promises are not binding on the court.

Can you notify your family of your arrest?

You have the right to make one phone call, within city limits. But, since you are only allowed one phone call, you must decide whether to call your family or your lawyer. Your request, however, must be granted promptly.

When you are arrested and booked, what happens to the money and personal property that you are carrying?

The police can take it temporarily, but they must give you an itemized receipt for all money and personal property taken from you.

Can you be released on bail to wait for trail?

You have the right to apply for bail. (The purpose

of bail is to make sure that you will appear in court on trial date.) For minor offenses, the police may release you on bail. In other cases, a judge fixes the amount of bail. You have the right to be brought before the judge without unnecessary delay in order to have the amount of bail determined.

How is the amount of bail determined?

Constitutionally, bail is considered too high if it is larger than the amount necessary to make sure you will appear in court. This depends on how much money you have. The following factors are supposed to be taken into consideration:

1. Whether the offense is a felony or only a misdemeanor.

2. The character and reputation of the defendant, including criminal record, if any.

3. The financial assets of the defendant. (How much money must be tied up to keep the defendant from "skipping town.")

4. The employment status and record, if any. This shows whether this defendant is reliable and likely to stay put.

5. The family status and roots in the community. Family and roots may make it inconvenient to run away. (This does not often apply to minors who are unlikely to be married and have children; but their relationship with their parents or guardians will be taken into consideration.)

How should you act if you are innocent of what you are arrested for?

To resist a policeman is a crime—even if you are innocent. The officer also has the right to stop you under "suspicious circumstances"—and the policeman decides when the circumstances are suspicious. If you refuse to answer questions or to show identification, the officer may then arrest you for disorderly conduct, or for refusing to obey orders. Therefore, be cooperative. If you are arrested illegally, you can sue the policeman for false arrest. But if the arrest was lawfully made, your innocence does not entitle you to recover damages.

After arrest, when do you go before a magistrate?

After booking at the police station, you must be taken before a magistrate "without unnecessary delay." But, if a magistrate or judge is not in court, you may be held until the next court session (unless, of course, you obtain bail).

Should you have a lawyer with you when you do appear in court?

You certainly should. The court will advise you of your right to have a lawyer even if you do not have the money to hire one. The court must also tell you the charge against you and it must allow you a reasonable length of time to send for a lawyer. If you request it, the court must put off the hearing until you can get a lawyer and it must direct an officer to take a message to your lawyer without fee.

What else happens when you appear before a judge?

The judge holds a "hearing" at which witnesses are questioned. You have the right to testify if you wish. But you do not have to. You can ask that the hearing be postponed until your lawyer is present. For certain offenses (which vary with each state), this hearing amounts to a trial. The judge will decide the case himself and either dismiss the charge or find you guilty. Where the charge is of a more serious nature he can decide only whether or not there is a reasonable basis for accusing you of the crime. He cannot decide whether or not you are guilty. In such a case, you have the right to waive the hearing and request trial before the proper court. Generally, if you are charged with a felony (a serious crime), he will hold you for the grand jury.

What will the grand jury do?

It either will dismiss the charge against you or it will *indict* you, meaning that you must be tried in a trial court.

Is a police officer allowed to search you?

A police officer may not stop and search (frisk) you unless he has reason to believe that you have committed or are about to commit a crime. Police have been known to violate that rule. However, you should cooperate in such cases to avoid making the situation worse, and because any evidence the police seize in an unconstitutional search can't be used as evidence against you. Furthermore, you may find that you have grounds for a lawsuit against the police.

May the police search your living quarters without a search warrant?

Generally only under the following circumstances:

1. When an arrest is made with a legal warrant for arrest, the premises where you are arrested may be searched for weapons or evidence.

2. If you give your consent, no warrant is necessary and you have given up your rights under the Fourth Amendment.[5]

When is a search warrant issued?

A search warrant must meet the requirements of the Fourth Amendment. It can be issued only upon "probable cause" and must describe specifically what is to be searched or seized. It is supposed to be a legal procedure directed by the court to get specific evidence of a crime. If the accused person is not at home at the time of the search and seizure, the police can still go ahead. And if no one will let them in, the police may enter by force.

May a policeman stop your car and demand to search it?

A police officer may not search your car unless he has a warrant or reason to believe that a crime has been committed or is about to be committed. Again, as in the case of stop and frisk, police have been

[5] The Fourth Amendment states: "The right of the people to be secure in their persons, houses, papers and effects, against unreasonable searches and seizures, shall not be violated, and no warrants shall issue but upon probable cause, supported by oath or affirmation, and particularly describing the place to be searched, and the persons or things to be seized."

known to violate this rule. Although you should certainly object, you should not physically resist. Any evidence obtained in an illegal search is inadmissible; and you might have grounds for a lawsuit against the police officer.[6]

Is shoplifting a serious offense?

In most jurisdictions shoplifting is a crime, and here is what the law says about it:

> The shoplifting statutes vary widely in their provisions, but in general they permit the statutory offense to be established by proof of fewer elements than in the case of larceny. Thus, under various statutes, shoplifting does not require proof of felonious or criminal intent, asportation (carrying away), ownership of the goods, or want of consent to their taking. Some shoplifting statutes declare it a crime to wilfully take possession of goods in a store with the intent of converting them to the taker's own use without paying the purchase price, whereas others penalize the concealment of unpurchased goods, while still upon the premises, and it is quite common for such statutes to establish presumptions arising from the concealment of goods upon the person or elsewhere.[7]

This means that in many places you can be convicted of shoplifting without the hard proof that would

[6] The preceding discussion of arrest procedures is drawn from *Police Authority and the Right of the Individual* by Sidney H. Asch (New York: Arc Books, 1968), pp. 10–13, 68–75.

[7] *American Jurisprudence Second*, Vol. 50, Paragraph 50, p. 217.

be needed for, say, theft of money. If you conceal something you haven't paid for, you could be arrested even without leaving the store.

In shoplifting, does the value of the article, or articles, taken affect the type of sentence one could receive?

Yes, it does. Usually, stealing goods valued at $10 to $200 is "petty larceny," whereas stealing more valuable things is called grand larceny. Obviously, grand larceny involves a heavier sentence.

What does the charge of vagrancy mean?

Technically, the charge of vagrancy means loitering without visible means of support. In the dictionary, a "vagrant" is a "wanderer" or "tramp."

Although most vagrancy statutes have been thrown out as unconstitutionally vague, some states continue to have them and enforce them on occasion. Vagrancy charges are sometimes used against young hitchhikers.

CHAPTER NINE

The Doctor and You— Medical Rights and Restrictions

At the present time, the laws about your right to get medical treatment independently are in a state of confusion. And they vary from state to state. Formerly, there was far less confusion because minors had to have the consent of a parent or guardian to get any medical treatment.

Minors' rights to independent medical care are limited for two reasons. First, to protect minors from immature decisions of their own and from adult exploitation. And second, to protect the physician. A doctor may be sued for treating or operating on a minor without parental consent. For example, minors, on achieving their majority, could sue a doctor who had treated them, or who had operated on them, if the minors later disapproved of the treatment. In addition, a doctor could be charged with malpractice and/or assault and battery.

Now, attitudes about the medical rights of minors are changing. The following excerpt from a law journal illustrates a new awareness:

> It becomes evident that a person having the status of a minor may be hindered considerably in seeking medical care and treatment for a variety of reasons, not the least of which will be common law

rules that were originally developed to protect him from his own lack of understanding and experience. It is widely recognized that children and youth do not play the same role in modern society as in the past, and that minors have health care needs beyond those to which their parents are willing to subscribe. It seems necessary, therefore, to move by legislation in the direction of granting minors a power of decision adequate to bring within their reach the medical care they seek independently of their parents' knowledge or consent. It is quite possible that such a power of decision may find its support in rights of privacy and autonomy granted by federal and state constitutions to minors equally with other persons under the law. The fear, of course, is that giving such a prerogative to underaged persons would disrupt the family as a unit of society. The doctrine of parental consent may have limited usefulness in shoring up the family unit, but a multitude of other legal devices exist that more adequately serve to protect the relational interests of the family members.[1]

Further on, the article gets more specific:

A number of proposals have been made for legislation enabling minors to seek health services in their own right. State legislatures have moved into this field with deliberate speed, some granting rights to minors piecemeal, some through comprehensive legislation. At least one state has completely abolished the requirement of parental consent to medical

[1] *Oklahoma Law Review,* Spring 1977, pp. 386–387.

treatments of minors. Several states now permit minors to give blood to voluntary noncompensatory blood programs without the need of parental consent. Virtually every state now has some provision whereby minors may seek treatment for venereal disease, and several states have enacted similar provisions which address other acute health needs, such as drug dependency, tests for pregnancy, and treatment for alcohol abuse. Regardless of the content of these specific statutes giving youths a mandate to seek treatment for particular health problems, the overriding legislative policy in almost all cases seems to be the same as that expressed by the Louisiana legislature when it resolved:

(T)hat the provisions and terms of said [health care for minors] Acts be liberally construed and applied in order to achieve the general purpose of said measures, namely, to enable Louisiana's minor citizens seeking medical care, related services and advice to receive the highest degree of such medical care, related services and advice as is possible from licensed physicians, hospitals, public clinics, all in order to actively and positively encourage the betterment of the health of the citizens of our state.[2]

However, the change is slow. Here is how a current medical reference book for the legal profession describes the situation.

The general rule is that an operation upon a

[2] *Ibid.,* p. 388.

minor requires the consent of the parent or guardian except in an emergency when immediate treatment is imperative and delay involves serious risk to the patient. However, in cases involving minor children sufficiently mature to understand the nature and consequences of the operation, and in cases involving simple procedures, the courts have often refused to invoke the rule requiring parental consent.

. . . Some courts have held that the minor's consent is sufficient if he is mature enough to understand the full significance of the contemplated treatment.

. . . The prudent physician should, as a general rule, obtain the consent of a parent or legal guardian before performing elective surgery or medical treatment upon a minor.

. . . Considering the unsettled nature of the law, a reasonable safeguard in all elective cases is to obtain the written consent to surgery of any minor child over fifteen years of age, in addition to that of the parents.[3]

The law is indeed "unsettled" in this field and the text is full of conflicting cases. In one case, two adult sisters took an eleven-year-old child to a hospital to have badly diseased tonsils and adenoids removed. The child died while under the anesthetic. The case went to court, which held that the child's father could recover damages from the operating surgeon because there was no immediate emergency that allowed for the absence of parental consent.

[3] R. C. Morris and A. Moritz, *Doctor and Patient and the Law* (4th ed.; St. Louis: C. V. Mosby Company, 1970), p. 161.

But in another case, an eighteen-year-old girl (a minor under her state's statutes) was judged capable of giving consent to a simple operation involving plastic surgery. And a seventeen-year-old boy was adjudged capable of giving consent to a smallpox vaccination, "because he had sufficient intelligence to know what he was doing."

Let us now try to answer some specific questions.

Can you request medical treatment from a doctor on your own initiative?

You can try. But because of the legal risk, most physicians will not treat you without your parent's permission. Also, a doctor may be afraid he won't be paid.

Can a female minor obtain an abortion without parental consent?

It depends upon the state where she lives. The law of the land is that a female has the right to an abortion during the first twelve weeks of pregnancy (see chapter 3). However, some states still refuse to accept this. For information, counseling and referral on abortions, you may contact Planned Parenthood League. They are able to advise you on local regulations and the location of abortion clinics.

Can you refuse to submit to treatment or to an operation which your parents or guardian wish you to undergo?

In many cases, a surgeon will not perform an operation without the minor's consent. And ordinarily a physician won't treat you against your will, because when you attain your majority, you may be able to bring suit against him.

Can you be sterilized—to prevent your having children—without parental consent?

Generally, the consent of both parents or guardians, *and* the minor is required by a doctor.

If you are injured, will a hospital treat you without parental consent?

Minors will not be treated unless the injury is so severe that delay may be fatal. As a recent example, a fifteen-year-old boy who had cut his hand badly went to the emergency room of a New York City hospital accompanied by his parents. His hand was treated and stitched. He returned alone a week later to have the stitches removed, but the hospital refused to treat him because his parents were not with him.

Can minors be confined to a hospital for mental illness, without their consent?

Here, the same rules apply to minors as to adults, although these laws are also in a state of confusion. In general, the prevailing legal situation is that minors, like adults, can be confined to a mental institution against their will—providing all the conditions of state law are met. These laws are often vague and each case may be handled differently. The following passage gives some idea of the thicket of special provisions and situations that exists:

Even though under the common law any person

has the right to detain a dangerous mentally ill person, the absence of special provisions creates numerous problems:

1. Detention is permitted only of dangerous persons found at large, but no mentally ill person may be removed from his home without a warrant.

2. Many officers are reluctant to detain a mentally ill person if such action is not specifically authorized by statute.

3. Mentally ill persons detained under the general police power are usually kept in jail. Such action is strongly disapproved of by hospital authorities and other groups interested in the welfare of the mentally ill.

In all states having emergency detention legislation an application is required in order to begin the proceedings. Some states authorize any reputable citizen to file the application; others recognize as applicants only law enforcement or health officers or a member of the family.

Although detention is usually delegated to the police or other administrative officers, judicial approval is still necessary in many states. In others only medical certification is required. Usually, the power to certify is not limited to psychiatrists but is granted to all physicians.

To prevent abuses several states require that the medical examination on which the certificate is based be made no more than 3 days prior to the date of the certificate.

Specific limits on the length of emergency detention are included in most laws, inasmuch as the detention is justified only until proper legal steps can be taken for hospitalization. The usual period is between 5 and 10 days, although the range is from 48 hours to 30 days.

The Special Committee on the Rights of the Mentally Ill of the American Bar Association stated that emergency commitment "should be for a period of not longer than seven days in any instance . . . at the termination whereof the patient should be discharged unless . . . appropriate steps have been taken for prolonged hospitalization." [4]

This refers to temporary, emergency detention. In those states where there is no emergency detention legislation, one can be hospitalized as follows:

. . . The procedure most favored by the critics of judicial hospitalization is hospitalization on medical certification, which is best exemplified by Section 6 of the Draft Act which is set out below.

(a) Any individual may be admitted to a hospital upon

(1) written application to the hospital by a friend, relative, spouse, or guardian of the individual, a health or public welfare officer, or the head of any institution which such individual may be, and

(2) certification by two designated examiners that they have examined the individual and that they are of the opinion that

(a) he is mentally ill, and

(b) because of his illness is likely to injure

4 *Ibid.*, p. 203.

himself or others if allowed to remain at liberty, or

(c) is in need of care or treatment in a mental hospital, and because of his illness, lacks sufficient insight or capacity to make responsible application therefor.[5]

Is what you tell your doctor confidential?

There is no definite answer. If minors suffer from a communicable disease and there is danger of their infecting others, the doctor may have a duty to warn others of the dangers of the case. Although most doctors will not release medical information about adult patients without the patients' written consent, the exception may be in releasing it to parents who are responsible for the minors.

The treatment of venereal disease is usually on a confidential basis—often in special clinics set up for this purpose. For a further discussion of VD see chapter 3.

[5] *Ibid.,* p. 204.

CHAPTER TEN

The Right of Minors to Hold Public Office

Who may be elected, or appointed, to public office? Theoretically, any person who is eligible to vote may hold public office whether it be national, state, or municipal. This would seem to include voters aged eighteen. But this is not the case. Why? Because in many states, although eighteen-year-olds may vote, they are still legally classified as minors, and different states have different rules about whether minors can hold public office. This situation is presently causing some confusion in the United States.

Many public offices have age limitations which have nothing to do with the age of minority or majority. Thus, to be eligible to be President of the United States, one must be thirty-five or over. A United States Senator must be thirty, and a Representative must be at least twenty-five. Each state has its age specifications regarding various positions in public office. Municipalities also have theirs, so that some cities allow an eighteen-year-old to be mayor (where this happens to be the age of majority).

At any rate, for minors in general, here is how a law encyclopedia describes the general position.

At common law infants are eligible to offices which are ministerial in their character [this means performing routine governmental functions which do not require personal judgment] and call for the exercise of skill and diligence only, but they are not eligible to offices which are judicial, nor should offices imposing duties to the proper discharge of which judgment, discretion, and experience are necessary be entrusted to infants. In accordance with these rules it has been held that an infant may be an appraiser of land to be sold on execution, an overseer of a public road, or a deputy county clerk. On the other hand, it has been held that an infant cannot act as a deputy sheriff or a constable.[1]

Stripping the above of polite and legalistic language, it says that, because minors are lacking in both experience and mature judgment, they may hold only those public offices that require nothing more than basic skills. However, just how and where to draw the line is left in a state of limbo.

For eighteen-year-olds, the situation is described as follows: (Note that many state constitutions provide for specific age requirements for important offices.)

With respect to public office holding by eighteen-year-olds, it may be noteworthy that the first four states to lower the voting age retained an age requirement of at least twenty-one for office holding.

Where age for office-holding is not specified in the Constitution, the lowering of the voting age may also lower the office-holding age. Frank J. Kelley, Michigan Attorney General, rendered an opinion that

[1] *Corpus Juris Secundum,* Infants, Vol. 43, Paragraph 24, p. 85.

stated, "Persons who are not qualified to vote for a particular office are ineligible to hold such office." The opinion was based upon Attorney General v. Abbott, 121 Michigan 540 (1899). In Ohio, the Secretary of State has advised Board of Elections, "unless the Ohio Revised Code or Constitution provides a specific exclusion from eligibility to run for state office for a given office seeker, he would be eligible to run if eligible to vote. Since eighteen-year-olds are now 'electors' under present Ohio law, they are not excluded from elective or appointive office by reason of age." Lee Johnson, Oregon Attorney General, has held that a "registered eighteen-year-old may serve as an official registrar of voters unless prevented by some inherent disability arising out of his status as a minor." [2]

Today, since all of the states have lowered the voting age to eighteen, some of the confusion has been resolved. Minors below the age of eighteen remain subject to all the minority restrictions pertaining to the holding of public office in their state, since they are not eligible to vote. You probably cannot hold office or at best you can hold a basic "non-judicial" office (see quote on pages 146–147).

If you are 18 you must find out: 1. whether your state regards you as a minor and what restrictions it puts on you; 2. whether the office you seek carries a specific age limitation. To find the answers, inquire at your town hall or county clerk's office.

[2] *The Age of Majority* (Lexington, Ky.: Council of State Governments, 1972), p. 23.

SELECTED
BIBLIOGRAPHY

American Jurisprudence Second. Rochester, N.Y.: The Lawyers Co-operative Publishing Co., 1972.

Asch, Sydney H. *Police Authority and the Rights of the Individual.* New York: Arco Publishing Co., 1967.

Brenner, J. H. *Drugs and Youth.* New York: Liveright, 1970.

Corpus Juris Secundum. St. Paul, Minn.: West Publishing Co., 1972.

Nolte, M. C. *Guide to School Law.* West Nyack, N.Y.: Parker Publishing Co., 1969.

Remmlein, M. K. *The Law of Public School Administration.* New York: McGraw-Hill, 1953.

Simpson, A. H. *Infant and Servant.* London: 1909.

Stetler, C. and Moritz, A. *Doctor and Patient and the Law* (4th ed.). St. Louis: C. V. Mosby Co., 1970.

INDEX